WWII through the eyes of a child

The true story by Monique Raguet/Jones during the Nazi Occupation of France

*** The True Story of Monique Raguet/Jones ***

WWII through the eyes of a child. The true story by Monique Raguet/Jones during the Nazi Occupation of France is published by Monique Jones P.C. All written, Photographed and/or illustrated material, in whole or in part herein is the sole property of Monique Jones P.C. and Monique Jones.

All rights reserved under the International and Pan American Copyright Conventions.

Monique Jones P.C. is solely responsible for the printing, layout and formatting of this material. Distribution of this text and material herein, including but not limited to text, photographs and /or illustrations by photoplay or copy in whole or in part without prior written consent of Monique Jones P.C. is strictly forbidden and prohibited by international law.

Monique Jones P.C. and Monique Jones make no affirmations to the information and claims provided by some submissions.

Brief quotations from this book are allowable without special permission, provided that the accurate acknowledgment of the source is made. Requests for permission for extended quotation from or reproduction of this manuscript in whole or in any part may be granted with permission obtained from the author.

WWII through the eyes of a child. The true story by Monique Raguet/Jones during the Nazi Occupation of France

Monique Jones P.C. and Monique Jones

1st printing - Copyright – 2016 - Printed in U.S.A.

*** WWII Through the Eyes of a Child ***

Table of Contents

Introduction   5

Chapter 1: Portrait of Verdun   6
Chapter 2: Childhood   23
Chapter 3: The War Breaks   38
Chapter 4: The Evacuation   48
Chapter 5: During the Evacuation   58
Chapter 6: Back home   67
Chapter 7: Living Conditions   81
Chapter 8: Other civilians   92
Chapter 9: Trading food for Transportation   96
Chapter 10: Survival from starvation   99
Chapter 11: Holy Communion   101
Chapter 12: German Occupation   106
Chapter 13: Danger for our family   109
Chapter 14: Prisoners of War coming home   113
Chapter 15: Our feeling regarding to Germans   115
Chapter 16: Air Raids   119
Chapter 17: Liberation   132
Chapter 18: Return of American Troops   163
Chapter 19: My wedding and time in France   173

To Marsha.

Merci

Monique M. Raguet Jones

*** The True Story of Monique Raguet/Jones ***

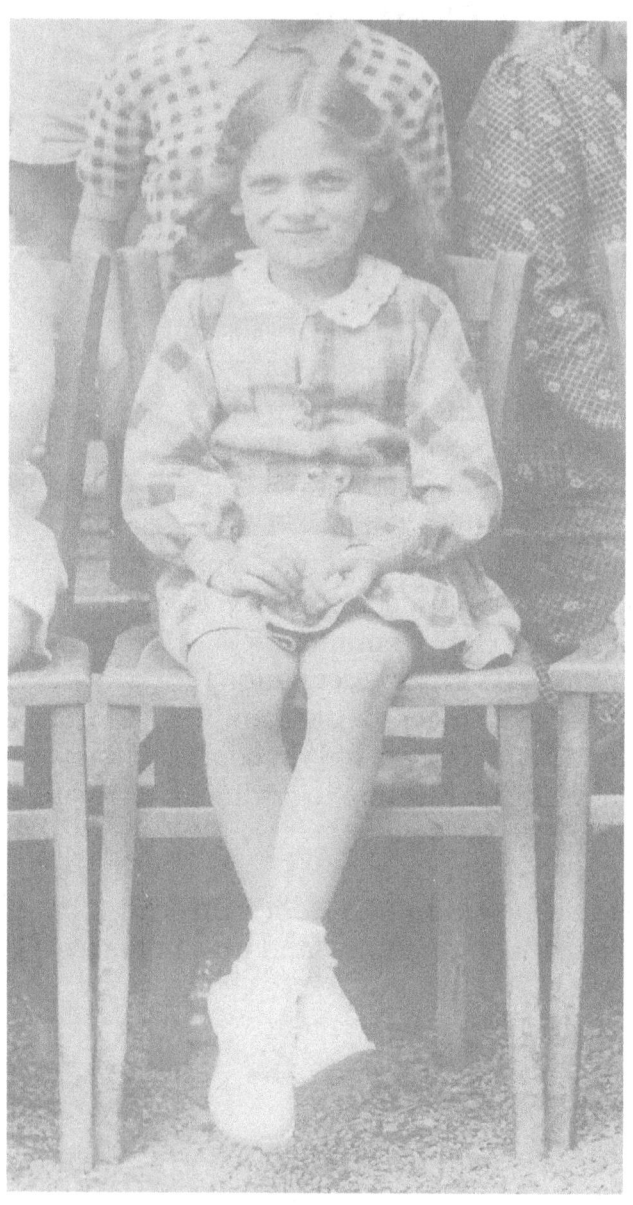

First Grade

Introduction

When you are born, everything is beautiful and miraculous. You are certainly not prepared for the challenges that life has to offer: the good things and the bad, the good times and the atrocities. But whatever life throws at you, it strengthens your character one way or another and builds your faith and courage.

I was born in late March 1931 at my home on 39 Quai de Londres in Verdun, which is located in the Lorraine province of Eastern France near the border of Germany, Belgium and Luxembourg. This very historical town was always bursting with pride over the centuries. It was the most hated place by Hitler during WWII. The Germans failed to take it during the First War, so he was driven by revenge. I grew up here during the Second World War, and as a child, I've seen the Germans occupy my town, I've seen the Americans come to liberate us, and I've seen all the horrors that war brings.

This is my life story; I wish to share it with you.

Chapter 1: Portrait of Verdun

Verdun is the second most historical town in France behind Paris. Among the things that make it so special are its many monuments. Of these monuments, a few particularly stand out. The most impressive and beautiful piece of architecture among them, located in the front of the cemetery, is called Douaumont, which was built in 1932 by the architects Leon Azema, Max Edrier and Jacques Hardy. It is interesting to note that America paid for a portion of this monument.

The Monument of Douaumont contains the bones of unknown soldiers who are buried there. The shape of the monument represents a sword hilt, with the blade planted in the ground in honor of the fallen heroes. The monument stands proud, protecting the grounds with its handle toward the sky and the sword buried with them, daring the enemies to disturb a peace so well deserved. No matter where you stand at this poignant memorial, you are at the center of the crosses. You are their surviving heroes, and they honor you with the ultimate sacrifice: their lives, so that we could live in peace.

La Citadelle or Les Ramparts de Verdun, (*pictures pages 10, 31, 32*) which I will refer to later on, was built in 1552. It was a fortified underground town. Having survived several wars, the fortress was impenetrable—a stronghold with shooting galleries, gun chambers, and numerous tunnels going into many directions. Les Ramparts are located on the outskirts of Verdun at the other end of town (refer to picture later in book). The cathedral of Verdun was where I was baptized and made my First Holy Communion. Though not as glamorous or prestigious as some of the other Cathedrals in France, it has a wealth of history behind it.

During the First World War between 1916 & 1917, bombs destroyed a massive part of the eastern corner and one of the steeples of Notre Dame de Verdun. To this day, one of those steeples has never been rebuilt. Through the impact of the bombs, some catacombs from 330 A.D. were unknowingly discovered. As a child, I remember looking at the pillars and could hardly make out the carving of people on the columns because they were so old.

The steps were even worn out from the passage of the Christians. The crypt was built during the Roman Empire and was restored during the period from 1920 to 1936, when the Cathedral was re-inaugurated. The altar is a replica of St. Peter's Basilica in Rome. The crypt is used for morning masses, catechism, religious classes, and private meditations. First Holy Communion, Confirmation, weddings, and other sacraments are officiated in the above ground cathedral with a majestic altar, three-story high organ, beautiful stained glass windows, and gothic architecture. The church was spared during WWII. The seminary is separated from the main church by a courtyard.

All my life, a certain religious event stood out in my mind that I spoke of from time to time. I was in the choir along with other children. The mass lasted 5 to 6 hours, during which we saw many bishops and cardinals. It was like pageantry, but as a fasting child, it seemed like an eternity. For those familiar with the Catholic religion, when there is such an elaborate display of the Princes of the Church, the details of the ceremony are very lengthy and precise.

Among the bishops was Msgr. Roncalli (*future Pope John XXIII*), who came to crown Notre Dame de Verdun in July 1946. It made such an impression that I now know why being in the presence of a future Pope was so exceptional.

We lived in a very nice community. Across the street from us was Le Quai, which is a park that has some benches and trees but mostly hard sand and very little grass. This is very common in France, especially bordering rivers, and we just happened to live next to the river. On the other side of the river was another street, La Rue de la Republique, where there was a bank, the officers' club, and a spa. They were all beautiful buildings. Just around the corner, one block from our house on the Quai de Londres was the post office where my dad was the postmaster, along with a bank, a four star hotel, a movie theater, and some other stores. The house my family owned was a beautiful and upper-class sidewalk café built with stones. It is located at the corner of Quai de Londres and Rue Edmund Robin in the middle of downtown Verdun near the river. A typical house in the city, it is four stories high with real functional wood shutters and no back yard, as it is against another business.

The first floor was the sidewalk café, surrounded by large windows on three sides. Two double doors, one facing Rue Edmund Robin and the other on The Quai de Londres, would open wide onto the terrace. At night, we would protect the pane glass windows with shutters, which were extremely heavy but retractable. They were hidden in a wood panel on each side of the windows. We would place a bar across the middle of the *volets* (shutters) when we closed the windows for the evening. The shutters were held by sturdy enormous hooks and pierced in the center. Heavy bolts would be inserted from the outside to the inside through those holes and reinforced with another pin crosswise inside.

From spring until late fall, we would open the doors on the patio. We had marble top tables and rattan chairs, and in between each set of tables were flowers in large containers. Yews gave privacy from one table to another. The patio was covered with a retractable awning, white with blue stripes facing the Quai, and umbrellas in each table on the Rue Edmond Robin's side.

Through a door in the back of the café were our kitchen and a bathroom. On the second floor were two bedrooms with fireplaces and a bathroom. On the third floor was our formal dining room and living room. From that hallway, a door would take us up one flight of stairs to the attic, where a large sunroof shed light.

Below the kitchen was our underground cellar where we stored wine bottles and barrels of beer and wine. Having a very solid foundation, it survived the first war. We had access to it by a double door that opened from the inside and was located in the end corner of the kitchen.

In France, people from all ages go to a café to relax, not to drink excessively, but the philosophy is that you order a beverage, whether coffee or alcohol, wine or a soft drink, then sit on the sidewalk, if possible, and enjoy each other's company. It is an overall friendly atmosphere. Some cafés serve blue-collar clientele, and others serve college professors, officers, lawyers, accountants, and upper-echelon citizens in general. Either type is good, but you choose the establishment most comfortable to you. This particular café was the center of my life and my only home until I came to the United States of America.

Verdun, France

The Ramparts and Citadelle of Verdun, the Cathedral are

the

Towers in the background

*** The True Story of Monique Raguet/Jones ***

France, my town is circled in red

The flag of Lorraine, France

My street in front of the River Meuse

My Grandma, Mom, and Arlette in the house in Briey the Kaiser stayed in

Mes Grandparents, Maman, and me

My mother and my uncle playing badminton (in the background is the famous bridge and "La Tour Chaussee," entrance to Verdun, located on the Meuse River)

My Mother to whom I dedicate this book

My sister in the background smacking me

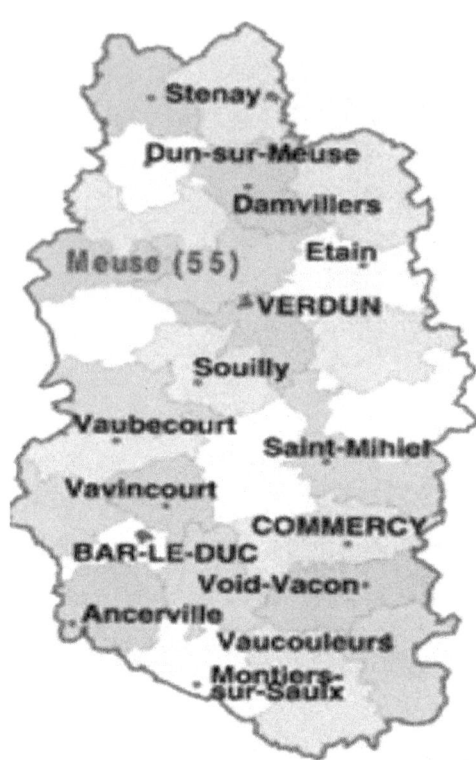

Department of Meuse
(one of 90 departments)
Part of Lorraine

*** WWII Through the Eyes of a Child ***

L'ossuaire (bone catacomb) de Douaumont

Le Monument des soldats aux Morts (Memorial to the Soldiers) near Pont Chausse

*** The True Story of Monique Raguet/Jones ***

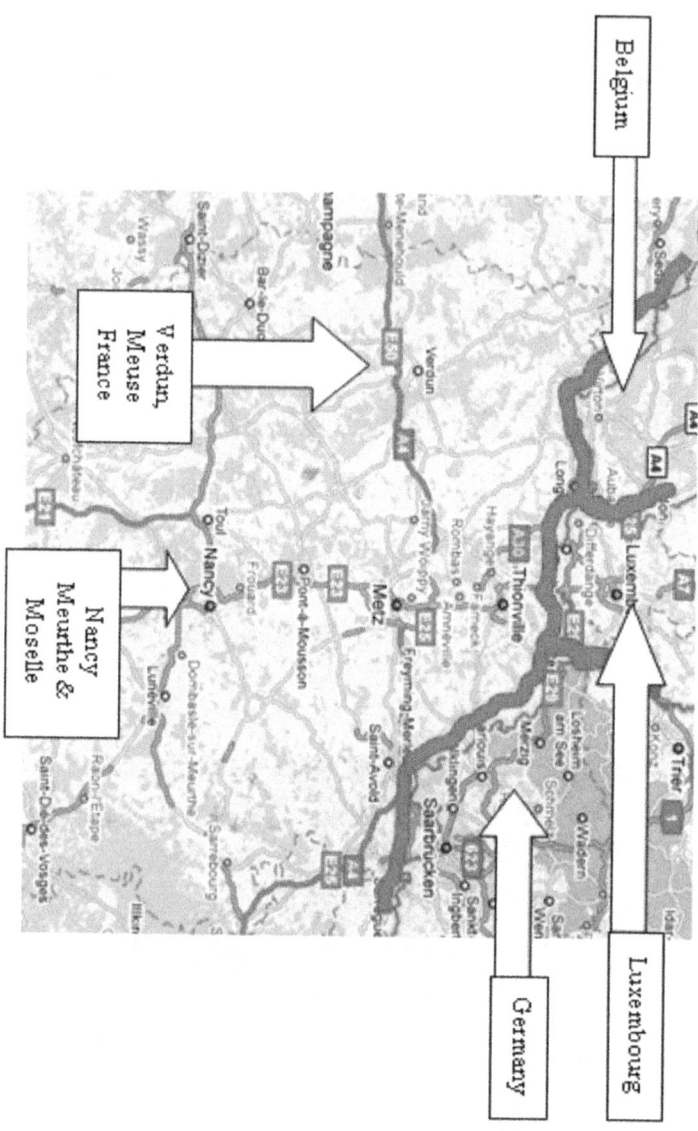

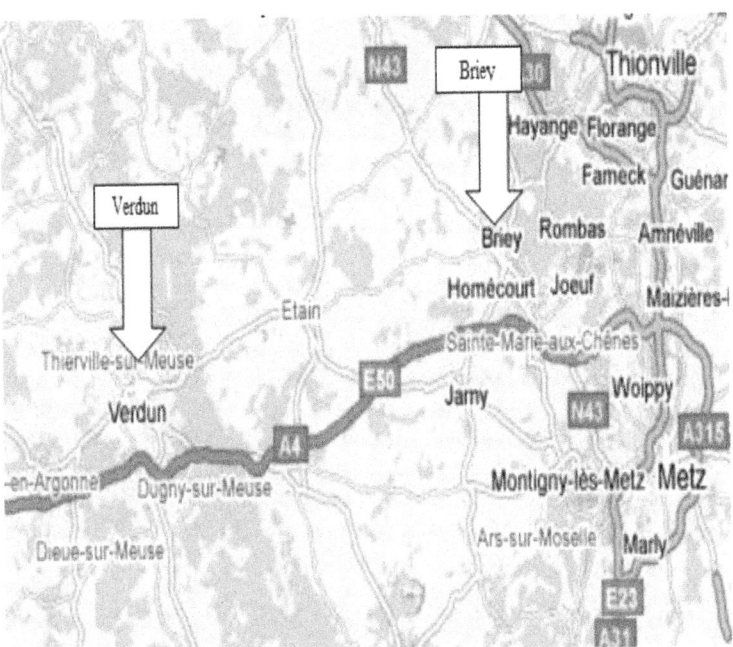

The Germans occupied Briey, but were stopped at Verdun during WWI

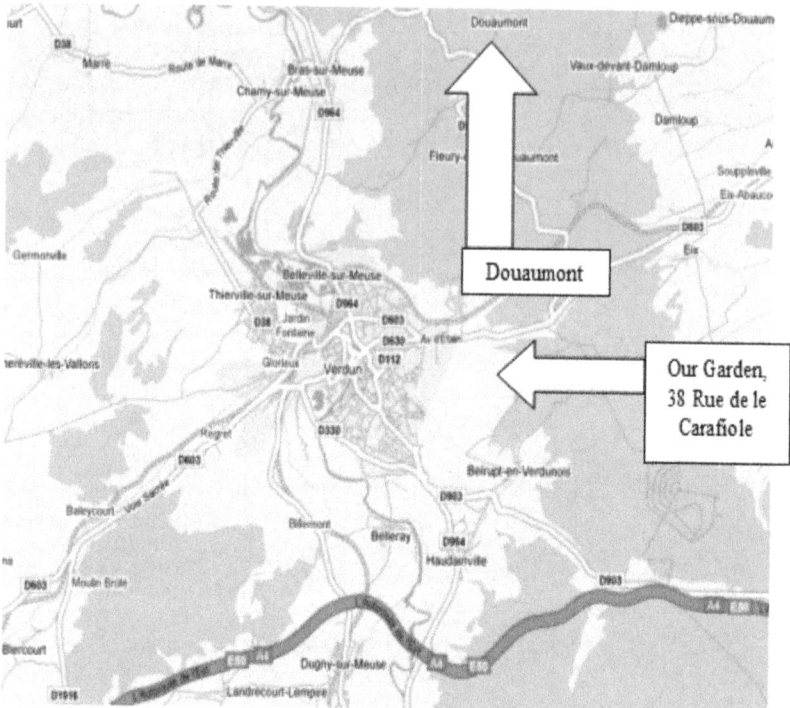

Map of the area near Verdun showing my family's garden and the Douaumont monument

Chapter 2: Childhood

My father, Jean Baptiste, was a very happy and typical southern Frenchman. He was born in the city of Pau near Bordeaux in the South of France. He was always full of life, an attitude vastly different compared to people born in the North of France, where wars broke out every 20 years. My mother, Germaine Esther, came from an area not far from Verdun, so she was considered a "Northern" Frenchwoman. She was very matter-of-fact since she lived through World War I when she was in her teens. The pressure she encountered during the war in 1914-1918 certainly didn't brighten her outlook. My mother was very proud of the fact she never smiled during the occupation! She made that clear during the First World War, when Kaiser Wilhelm II from Germany actually stayed overnight in my grandparents' house in Briey while he was reviewing the troops at the front. He chose their house because it was the best in the area. After his overnight stay, no other Prussians were allowed back in their home at all, in case the Kaiser decided to come back.

As for my siblings, I had one sister, Arlette, who was seven years older than me. When my mother was pregnant with me, my parents were expecting either "a rose" or "a cabbage." In France, this is a figure of speech. A rose means the child will be born with difficulty but will be beautiful nonetheless. A cabbage is a baby with an easy birth, but ends up, shall we say, not very attractive. In America, the "cabbage patch doll" was created from that idea.

As a rose has many thorns, I ended up being a rose for my parents during my birth. My mom was in a coma for three days after my delivery. She was unable to see me or nurse me until she recovered, a few days later. Our private physician had to use forceps to bring me out because I was born in a breach position. As a result, the instruments damaged part of my forehead and ears. By the time my mom recovered, I looked much more presentable as the doctor tried to mend the damage that was done. I was named Monique, which means counselor. What a dramatic start in life.

Growing up before the war, I was an extraordinary child. I would continuously dance like a ballerina on my toes, and our friends would even come over and watch. My best friend, Josianne, would visit everyday and we would dance together. She was the daughter of a beauty salon owner just two doors down from my house.

I did extremely well throughout school. I received the Presidential Award for outstanding scholastic achievement in first grade, a very rare and prestigious award. Madame Chevalier was the most exceptional teacher I ever had throughout all my school years and became my favorite. She was my role model, even though I only had her during primary school. We always kept in touch, and she even visited my parents once in a while.

Sadly, I wasn't very healthy as a child, which later became a cause of concern for my parents when we had to evacuate during the German occupation because I was vulnerable. I was skinny and my first set of teeth was black due to the lack of calcium. They were so bad the dentist had to pull them out. I never smiled in my old pictures because Maman (Mom) used to tell me, "Don't open your mouth when you smile or your black teeth will show." I am fortunate the second set came in perfectly white and straight.

That summer, I became so ill that I passed out in my parents' arms. The illness got progressively worse for me and lasted one year. Our personal physician, Dr. Bertrand, made house calls everyday. My family put together a makeshift bed for me in the kitchen on the table located in the back of the café. I was confined here all day long with no one to keep me company.

My friends from school, Jean Claude, Jeanine, and Josianne came every evening after class, bringing schoolwork from that day and we would do our homework together.

"Monique, I am so worried about you," my friend said. "Isn't the doctor helping you any? You are not looking any better. You look so tired."

"He does not know what is wrong," I replied. For a while, I continued to do my schoolwork until I eventually became too weak.

I spent most of my time with a coloring book and became friends with a hippo character named Zamzime. He used to live in the Congo, but now lived with me. He was my sole companion for a long time. I pretended we used to swim together and have a healthy, wonderful time. We had no worries then; he was an orphan, but now I was his friend. Together we escaped our fears: he, the beasts, and me, Dr. Bertrand's shots or unpleasant visits. That coloring book and my friend will be in my thoughts the rest of my life.

My parents finally moved me into the bedroom on the second floor, where we had a marble fireplace. On the mantle were two bronze statues; one is a farmer holding a fork, the other, his wife holding a rake and a bundle of hay under her left arm. The details are similar to a Michelangelo work of art.

We also had an ornate gold clock from Louis XIV's era that chimed every hour. On each side of the antique clock's pendulum were two porcelain dolls, one of Louis XVI and the other of Marie Antoinette. They were two extraordinarily detailed pieces of Limoges. Both were lavishly dressed in bright colored silks. They had such perfect faces and long wigs, they looked like real miniature humans, and the details on their visages made them appear even more realistic. Marie had blue eyes that matched her dress and proudly held her chest high.

The Bronze Statues

With nothing else to do while confined to my bedroom, I would stare at the statues, the dolls, and the fire in the hearth hour after hour while listening to the sounds of the old clock. From time to time, I had even had visions of a beautiful lady holding roses who appeared and spoke to me, calming my fears and giving me strength and hope. She was Sainte Therese. I felt her protecting me day after day, and as I would speak to her, my strength slowly returned.

One morning Dr. Bertrand came and announced, "Madame Raguet, I have good news. We discovered what is causing Monique's illness. She has trouble with her digestive system."

"Mon Dieu! merci (Thank you, my God)!" exclaimed my mother with happiness.

The doctor prescribed some medicine for me and my health slowly began to improve. It was like a miracle, and I started eating a little at a time. My illness lasted around eighteen months.

When I regained my health, I returned to school, where I excelled in every subject once again, even though I lost so much time.

"Mon Jesus, merci, my little girl is fine now," my mother said to my father one day when I was feeling better. "Jean, we are going to take Monique to the Stations of the Cross to thank God for her recovery."

"Are you out of your mind?" my dad said. "She will not make the trip—she is too weak yet!"

"I don't care—He protected her before, and He will do it again," she replied.

"We will take the bus early tomorrow morning and return tomorrow night. It is a miracle she is still alive."

We departed for the Stations early in the morning, but during the trip, the skies clouded up, and it rained the entire day. We were sopping wet even before we boarded the bus. We traveled with some other pilgrims to a little village. We walked up a hill, and stopped to pray at each Station of the Cross. The chanting of those devout believers still did not stop the rain. I was soaked, but very cheerful inside and thankful to be alive. I was wearing wool socks since I could not afford to catch a cold. By the time we got home that evening, we were completely drenched. My inner ankles hurt due to the friction of my bones with my wool socks, which resulted in huge gashes because the wool was irritating the wounds.

"Monique, what's wrong with you? You are not walking right," my mom remarked. "Oh! Ma Chèrie! Come here my darling, what's that on your socks?" She noticed the blood on each of my ankles and removed those awful socks to see what was wrong. She immediately panicked when she saw the gashes. "Oh no, not again—I have to get our Doctor".

In her over-zealousness, she confined me to my bed for the rest of the day until our good doctor arrived to my bedside once again. That didn't bother me as much, as long as I had Sainte Therese to keep me company. She was my strength. Because she also suffered during her life, she was my heroine and I became very attached to her. I still have the scars on my ankles, but I thank God for allowing me to recover and to make that small pilgrimage to the Stations of the Cross. Even though God left marks on me, I was definitely blessed. Those scars serve as a reminder that He forever remains within me.

The Post Office on the left corner where my Dad was Post Master. In the back the Monument de la Victoire

Below, the "goose Steps" in front of the Monument de la Victoire, Hitler saluting the parade, sad day!

My school behind the Monument

*** WWII Through the Eyes of a Child ***

The Citadelle outside Verdun

*** The True Story of Monique Raguet/Jones ***

The interior of the Citadelle where we had to sleep during the Battle of Bastogne

The multiple hallways of the Citadelle

*** WWII Through the Eyes of a Child ***

The ramparts surrounding Verdun, part of the Citadelle

Underground artilleries against tanks

Chapter 3: The War breaks

War: Regardless of the age, the time, the location, the purpose, war means death. War means misery, despair, and loss of loved ones. Each age has a war that defines their time, their situation. In my case, it was World War II.

The First World War took place during the years 1914 through 1918. The bulk of the war, the western front, occurred near Verdun and the surrounding areas, which are mainly located in the Provinces that are headed by the Department of Meuse, France. "*Picture on page 35*" There were a total of 90 departments.

From February 21, 1916 to December 19, 1916, there were over 300 days and 300 nights of relentless horrifying combat. Nearly 26,000,000 bombs were fired from the artilleries, an average of six bombs per minute. It was estimated that 350,000 soldiers from each side were killed or missing during that period. The total casualties during the war numbered <u>800,000 soldiers</u>, making it the bloodiest war to date and an absolute carnage.

After the war, the French Government, under the advice of Maréchal Joffre (a Maréchal is the equivalent of a five-star General), built the Maginot Line from 1929 - 1936. This Line was to be a fortification constructed of concrete and steel in order to protect France from future aggression. Named after French Minister of Defense André Maginot, it was a line of concrete with tank obstacles, artillery casemates, machine gun posts, and other defenses. It stretched from Switzerland to Luxembourg and was located just several miles east of Verdun.

At the end of 1939, I started to hear my parents speak of Poland being invaded by the Germans, and even the news on the radio was all about this invasion. The soldiers of the "German Reich" were now beginning to discuss invading France next.

One day my mom was crying silently in the kitchen and Dad had his arms wrapped around her to console her.

"No, Jean, you cannot leave us," she cried. "They are not mobilizing you."

"I have to go, Germaine, I have no choice," he said. "I will be commanding a post in the South of France, but I really don't know when, or where, so do not panic."

Our French army was proud and did their best to keep apprehensions out of our minds, so they held magnificent parades with troops representing each of our colonies. "*How could we not win the war?*" I thought to myself as I watched in amazement. Since my father was an officer and the postmaster of Verdun, we sat among the dignitaries in the front row on a platform three quarters of the way down the steps of "**Le monument de la** *Victoire*" (Victory Monument, in the center of Town) "*Pictures pages 29 & 30)* as we proudly observed the parade. It was important to the French citizens to pay homage to the fallen heroes who saved their lives and demonstrated our strength.

My Father received The Legion d'Honneur from the President of France

La Legion d'Honneur

When we had these parades, they would last almost a half a day. We felt so proud and safe. They marched, heads held high, turning toward us when passing the reviewing stand. So precise and so well rehearsed were the French Legionnaires in blue, white and red uniforms with the capes over their shoulders. There were Polytechnics, the future admirals of the Navy, dressed in black uniforms, while St. Cyr cadets, wearing red with their coifs adorned with white plumes, were the future officers. Then, the colonies followed: the Algerians; the Tunisians; the Moroccans, with their turbans wrapped around their heads and a lamb as their mascot; and the grenadiers with tall red hats, the Comorian and a roaring lion sitting upright, which was scary in the back of a jeep.

(*pictures page 49*)

"Maman, he is not going to get out and eat us, is he?" I stammered.

"No," she replied, he is tied up with chains.

The parade then became more intense. The name of the street where the monument is located is La Rue Mazel, and running parallel is Le Quai de Londres. The Quai is a large empty park bordering the river, where all the regiments gathered prior to the défilé (parade). They would go to the next street and pass the Monument. The Arabs were an exception. They would gallop full speed from the Quai de Londres directly to la Rue de la Victoire, the street facing the monument toward us. They were dressed in black, riding white Arabian horses, stopping a few feet from the reviewing stand and shooting their rifles in the air. It was a stunning picture, reflecting power and beauty. I was so frightened I put my hands over my ears and eyes, hid behind my dad.

Then came the Chasseurs Alpin (*soldiers strictly deployed to the Alps Mountains*) in dark blue uniforms with a light yellow French horn insignia on their dark blue berets, worn slightly on the right side of their heads. Preceding them was a marching band with French horns and trumpets. The cadence was extremely fast, permitting the soldiers to take two steps to one of the normal infantry. The battalion was trained to march this way in order to walk in the Alps and Pyrenees Mountains, or other mountains dividing France and foreign countries. They were protecting us from bordering hostile territories, such as Italy, Germany, and Spain.

The Navy uniforms were mostly white with red and blue trimming, and on their berets was a little red pompom. Each girl had to touch it for good luck after the parade. Indochina was also represented, along with Congo and many other colonies, but the ones I am describing here were the different armies that most impressed a very young girl. At the end of the parade was the artillery, and the numerous tanks would stop, and point their guns at us to salute us. Up above were the airplanes from which the vapors bearing the colors of the French flag (blue, white and red) would escape. In between were numerous marching bands.

I was also privileged to see King George VI and Queen Mary with their daughters, the future Queen Elizabeth II ("Lilibet" was her nickname) and her sister, Princess Margaret, along with the King and Queen of Spain and different Shahs of Iran and Iraq. Verdun, as I mentioned earlier, was the second most important town to visit in France.

"Oh, look, Papa's the pigeons are flying!" I exclaimed. Everything was so beautiful and we felt so safe and happy.

Weapons Turret

During World War I, pigeons were used to deliver messages wrapped around their legs. My dad raised them and received an award from the President of France called "La Legion d'Honneur," (*Picture page 36*) the highest award received for serving the country. The male would be let out of the cage and would fly back to the female. Pigeons mate for life. It was the male who flew over us; after all, they were soldiers in their own way. When a pigeon returned to the nest, we would remove the ring around his legs and drop it into a special machine provided by the government. The machines had a clock installed inside the box, and the arrival time would then be recorded. Owners of the "pigeons voyageurs" and the machines were considered the resistance later on during the German regime and could get the death penalty. These were highly regulated exercises of war.

"Monique, let's go up to the attic see the new baby pigeons," my dad would say. I was thrilled because I knew he would show me how to suck a pigeon egg, taking a needle and puncturing a hole on each side. We would drink from a gourde, a pouch made of goatskin, used to hold liquid. He would put it over his shoulders and show me how to drink wine or water. It was our private and precious time together.

"Jean, *qu'est-ce que tu fais* (what are you doing)?" my mom would tell him. "You are teaching her such common habits." My mother was furious about the whole thing, as it was not lady like to behave in that manner.

One morning, I heard my mom cry, **"No, Jean, it can't be!"**

Suddenly, my father was called to serve the army in the South of France again. Everyone was talking about the Maginot line. It was only five to six miles from Verdun, thus, we were very apprehensive. I really did not understand the concept of war, as we did not own a television then.

One day, I heard my mom talking with Josianne's mother when she came to set her hair. She was one of the friends who helped me with homework and her Mother was our hairdresser. She came every morning to set my mother's hair.

"Madame Petit, did you hear the latest news about having to evacuate?" my mom asked her.

"Oui, Madame Raguet, my husband left for the front this morning," Josianne's mom replied. "I have to take my daughter and Charlie my youngest son with me. We have very little money and no car. I don't know what is going to happen to us."

My mom shook her head. Evacuating was something I knew she never wanted to do it. Closing our establishment was impossible. For me, it was going to be an adventure! I would not say this out loud, but I was happy inside because we were finally going away.

"Josianne, did you hear? We are going on a trip!" I whispered excitedly to her.

My friend, though, was more subdued. Like her mother, she was worried. "I know Monique! I hope we go someplace that is fun and go together."

Gas mask we carried

Chapter 4: The Evacuation

Despite how reluctant my mom was to evacuate, we did nonetheless. One day she announced, "*Mes enfants* (my children), it is time to pack. Monique, do not forget your name tag and gas mask. Arlette, help me pack two small bags and we will each carry one. Monique is too fragile to have one."

My poor mom hurried us to pack some basic essentials, but I don't recall what else we took. What I do remember the most is putting my name tag around my neck and carrying those horrible gas masks (*picture page 43*) I eventually learned the date was June 11, 1940.

At last, we were ready to leave. My father was already with the troops in the southern part of France at the time. I had no idea where because it was confidential information. So it was just my Mom, Arlette, and myself. We went to purchase train tickets at the railroad station, which was already blocked. However, we had acquaintances and were able to go through the line. I believe we were heading south, away from the Germans. On the *Quai* (railroad platform), we passed a few hysterical individuals who frightened me.

"Why are they screaming and pushing people around like this?" I asked. "Oh—there goes Josianne, her mother, and little brother!"

My mom was so preoccupied that she did not bother answering me.

"Can we go with the children and Madame Petit?" I begged.

"Monique, *tais-toi* (keep quiet)!" My Mother finally responded, holding my hand very tightly.

49

The tickets we purchased took us to a first class private compartment. Outside the station, everyone else walked, rode bikes, or drove motorcycles since cars were not in abundance at the time. There was a lot of commotion and confusion around me. Despite all of this, the most important thing to me was that we were going away.

"Maman, where are we going?" I inquired. "Did you see our friends? They are on the other platform."

"Monique," Arlette snapped, "we don't care where others go, the only thing that matters now is our lives."

I thought that was such a harsh remark at the time, but I later learned in a case of disparity like this, your own life comes first. Everyone else was worried about my health, but I wasn't.

It was exciting that we were now on a train instead of stuck in the house or in my bed. When the train left the station, I felt so lucky because I didn't have to walk or ride a bike like everyone else did.

I remember being told the train was seven miles long and was transporting wounded soldiers from the front line back to the South of France. Although our compartment was very comfortable, with velvet cushions; first class compartment; it was crowded. I can't remember the faces or how many surrounded us, as it was all a blur.

In our car were only civilians.

In France the trains have 3 different types of cars, first class, (which we occupied), Second class and third class where the wounded soldiers were travelling.

Right after leaving the station, the train was moving so slowly that a pedestrian could have kept up with us. We saw the injured soldiers walking alongside the train. How scary it was for a child to see those French heroes who once paraded proudly now covered in blood, staring at nothing, lost and defeated. Their heads hung down, and some were screaming with pain. Some resembled mummies with their heads all wrapped up, and others were holding one arm with the other. One young soldier, not much older than my sister, lost his leg, and another one with crutches was helping him to walk. One soldier in particular frightened me, part on his head had been missing, blood running down his uniform. They kept looking at us with pleading eyes. The horrible picture of war was unfolding before us. I was so young, but have never forgotten this bloody and horrifying vision. I've dreamed about it many times and even now I shiver at the images I was exposed to. All I kept thinking was how being confined to bed was nothing compared to the suffering of those poor human beings trying to defend my homeland and dying for my security. I knew it was all for this country, but I still felt somewhat responsible despite how young I was. They were martyrs, and here we were sitting in a comfortable cabin, I thought.

As we rounded a bend and entered a small valley, we saw on top of a hill what appeared to be nuns and priests running down toward us. Suddenly, we heard gunshots and shouting all around us. The people in our compartment removed the thick cushion seats and placed them against the windows as we lay down on the floor. No one made a sound. We were so frightened, we could hardly move. In this situation, you know if you scream, the enemy will find you and kill you. Your body betrays you in fear and its control kicks in. You are paralyzed and your mind goes numb. Survival instincts take over.

We later learned the nuns and priests were Italian soldiers in disguise who wanted to kill the wounded French soldiers. It was not the first time they tried to kill us. It happened later on during our trip! When the fighting was over the doors on the train opened, some French soldiers told us to come out. I remember, I was very thirsty and was crying for water. I still have this reaction when I get scared or nervous.

What I was not told was about how the enemies, who were trying to kill the wounded French soldiers, most of them, were finally massacred. My mom protected me from that vision. All I could think of was how thirsty I had been. The remaining French soldiers told us we were on our own because they had to tend to the wounded and the dead from the attack. We grabbed our things and left the train.

Soldiers' Uniforms

African troops

The French Foreign Legion

Polytechnics marching

After we exited the train, the three of us were alone again. I don't know what happened to the people who were in the compartment with us, as they scattered in different directions. We then had to walk. By the evening, we were fortunate to find a barn where we could spend the night. At that time hundreds of evacuees joined us. Noise and chaos were everywhere as we all crammed into the barn. The smell of fresh cut hay surrounded us. It was so overwhelming, but yet a home-like feeling. My mom was worried that my sister and I would get lice in our hair or fleas from sitting and sleeping in the hay. When I think back, we could have been shot or burned, with people smoking cigarettes and lying in the barn.

What a hazard, the building could have caught fire and yet she was more concerned about us getting lice or fleas! It became a personal family joke. People were packed in with us like it was a whole city. We huddled together in fear as we heard planes and gunshots surrounding the farm, but fortunately, we made it through the night. Even, now, so many years later, the smell of fresh cut hay still brings back memories of that night. Smell never leaves your mind, it is embedded in your brains.

1

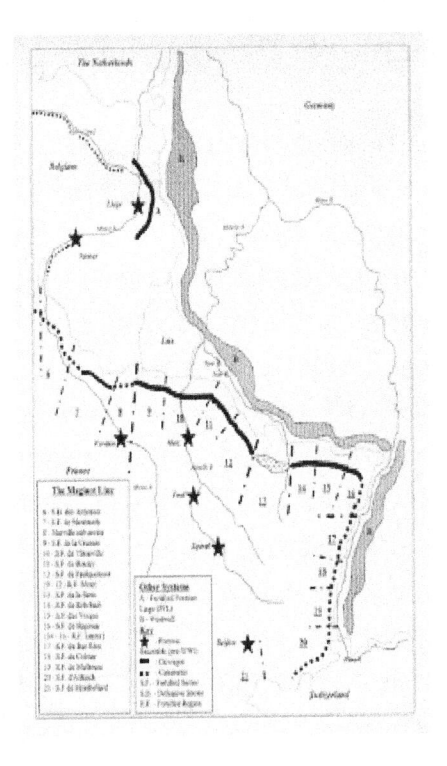

The Maginot Line, Verdun is the fifth star going upward. It is approximately several miles from Verdun

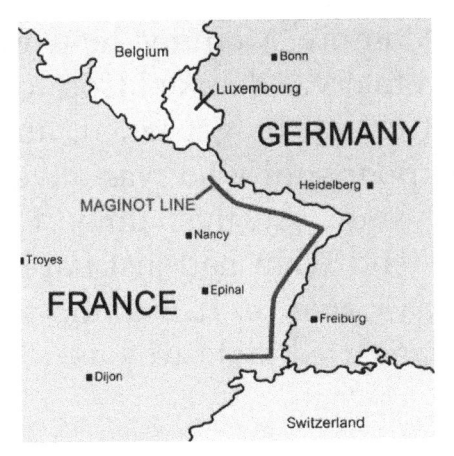

Chapter 5: During the evacuation

The next morning as dawn broke, we were back out of the barn and walking on the road again. Suddenly over the horizon, Italian warplanes flew over us, so close we could almost see the pilots. They swooped toward us. Arlette grabbed my hand and we jumped off the road into a small ditch. As the planes fired their machine guns down the center of the road, we could hear the bullets whistling by us. After the planes had passed, we got up, but the person who was lying beside me didn't move. I shook his shoulder and said, "You can get up now, it's over."

No response; he was dead.

"Mommy, Mommy, he won't get up!" I started to cry. I thanked God for saving us and not letting us get killed, and I prayed for this poor soul who was alive just a few minutes ago. At that time, I could not comprehend what had just happened; only later was I able to. It was the second time the Italians tried to destroy us!

We hit the road again. There was nothing to eat or drink; we just kept walking and walking, putting one foot in front of the other. The three of us walked with all those, strangers who had now become our brothers, sisters, even so we never had a conversation with them. I kept thinking about the deceased lady near me! What happened to her? How did she died, and why?

The second night we found a deserted little suburban house. The owners of the house had fled the Germans long before we did. The home was so pretty, an A-frame home, shaped with a solid chimney and pine trees in the front lawn. In the back were a stream and a garden full of roses and peonies. The air surrounding us was filed with such fragrant aroma. What a difference from the scent of the hay. It made us feel safe, alive, it was home again, my wonderful garden.

"Monique, go and pick flowers to put in a vase," my mom told me that day. "Also pick some strawberries, green onions, and radishes from the garden so we can eat them tonight."

I thought to myself, *"Why would she think of picking roses at a time like this?"* But it made us feel better.

The house was vacant, so some of us refugees stayed overnight in it. I went out and soaked my feet in the cool water of the stream, running in the backyard. I laid in the grass, tasting a blade, and wondering what happened to Josianne, Jean-Claude, and their families. Soon I was taking a little nap. It was quiet for the first time. Normal for a change, no rifles, explosions, screaming, chaos. I was actually able to sleep in a bed that evening. It was relatively peaceful and serene throughout the night.

Underground artilleries against tanks

At the crack of dawn, my mother woke us up and we started to move on. It was awful; I felt like I was leaving home again. I had a dream that night that I was back in Verdun, but now I had to get up and get back on the road with all those desperate strangers. Before our departure, my mother cleaned the furniture and made the beds. I couldn't believe it—here we are as refugees, and she is now trying to clean up the house we just used. While I thought it was strange at the time, looking back I now realize that you have to keep some order in your life by maintaining your habits, it keeps you sane. Routines are comforting in a way because they are a part of regular living. My Mother was so tired, but she was trying to bring back a sense of normality.

We got back on the road and continued walking. We split up with the people who had stayed with us. Too many large groups of evacuees were targeted easier, I didn't understand why.

"*Aurevoir* (goodbye), *bonne chance*," Maman told them. *Why didn't we stay together?* I wondered. New faces every day almost every hour! Old, young, scared, grumpy, crying, always making certain I followed my Mom and Arlette, that fear of getting lost.

As we walked, a farmer passed us and looked back at me. I guess he felt bad for me since I was so tired and so little with legs like toothpicks. He picked me up and let me ride on his horse-drawn wagon. I felt that I was ten stories high. My eyes always searching for my family. He had a huge wheel of Swiss cheese, very common in France, a country well known for its gourmet and numerous cheeses. The wheel was seven feet wide and one foot high. (At least it looked that way to me). It was encased in a thick, hard crust in order to keep it fresh. The farmer cut off a little piece with a very large knife and gave it to me to eat. It was Gruyere cheese, gold, full of holes, the most delicious, since I was starving. Again the smell and look of Swiss cheese reminds me how fortunate we are to be able to eat it so freely, in abundance. We were always hungry and thirsty.

My mother continuously worried about my sister Arlette and I, trying to keep us together, which was an enormous task in itself. The only thing that gave me any kind of comfort or peace of mind was the badge with my name and address I had around my neck I could not get lost! How innocent your mind is at that age. Anything could have happened, but I didn't realize the consequences, which was a blessing.

Another day, some other farmers placed me on a horse. *"Ma'am, this child has had it,"* they said. "Let her ride on my farm horse for a while."

"She never rode one before, so please watch her," my Mom told them, kind of worried.

My first experience on this enormous animal as tall as an elephant, in my eyes, was not pleasant, I got so nervous that I felt sick. For that reason, I am still scared of horses, that feeling never changed.

One day when we had stopped and were resting, we heard the news, the Germans had invaded France and our country had to surrender, what did it mean? How could this happen to us, the invincible, and all those soldiers we saw parading in a front of us only a few months ago? They seemed ready for the worst. Tears were running down the French people faces, what kind of future were we going to face?

We were now close to Dijon after walking all the way from Verdun, approximately 250 miles one way, always on foot, with complete strangers. I remembered the name of the town, due to the Mustard of Dijon, plus a liqueur served in our café, by the name of "Cassis", very strong, but sweet, made of currant (in the grape family). Everyone was in a daze, staring at nothing, depressed, but mostly mortified with shame we didn't know why we surrendered so quickly.

Again, my mommy did something that was very strange to me. She threw her bag to the ground and picked up a small pocketknife she had in it, and threw it away. She was afraid we would now be arrested with possession of arms and horrible things would happen to us. We were laughing at her, but we forgot that she had already been through the horrors of WWI and knew what was coming, so she wanted to protect us.

When we finally made it to the city of Dijon, the capital of the Department of Cote D'Or, as I explained mustard, cassis and champagne, the Germans were already waiting there. We were all shaking and petrified, we all thought they would shoot us on sight. However, they were very polite. They wore green uniforms, tight fitted helmets, shiny leather boots, and a belt with the inscription "*Gott mit uns*" (God be with us). I remember this because I was at eye-level with their waists at the time and kept staring at the buckles where the inscription was engraved. They were clicking their boots together to greet each one of us. Around their necks was a large piece of metal that was probably their name tags. They told us that we were to turn around and head back to our homes.

So we walked all the way back from Dijon to Verdun. I was not prepared for yet another horrible and permanent vision in my mind of passing columns after columns of French soldiers bleeding intensely, with their heads hanging low, hands above their heads, escorted by an enemies guards holding rifles. The sadness was piercing our hearts from the sight of our defeated army. It was unbelievable. We were looking at every soldier, hoping to see my dad, (impossible since he was in South of France) but yet deep down inside, we didn't want to see him there or someone else we knew. They were likely being escorted to German camps.

We made it home on June 21st, the feast day of Saint Jean Baptiste. *"Aujourdh'ui est la fête de votre Père* (Today is your Dad's feast day)," my mom wept quietly.

I was extremely exhausted and my thoughts of a vacation to the South of France were not what I had expected. It was the beginning of a long four years of occupation, hunger and suffering.

Chapter 6: Back Home

When we re-entered Verdun on June 21st, 1940, there were nothing but Germans all around, and we were shaking. We thought a lot of neighbors were already home, but as we got closer to town, all we saw were swastikas hanging from the *bâtiments* (buildings). A few young German soldiers, polite but with ice-cold facial expressions, came to greet us. "Madame, there are no civilians back yet; you are the first ones."

My proud mother answered, "I don't care, I want to go home. Look at my little girl, she can hardly walk. She will die if we stay one more day out here."

"Where do you live?" The stern soldier asked.

"*39 Quai de Londres, across the river,*" Arlette answered. You can see our house from here.

"The bridge named *Pont Pointcaré* is demolished, so we will have to carry the child. Both of you have to cross the Meuse River on the makeshift bridge."

"We will; we have come so far; we can master this; trust me," she said.

I thought these Germans were very polite. They gave us a guard to escort us back to our house, since we were the first and only French civilians re-entering Verdun.

"Follow him and no trouble," called the guard, clicking his heels. He must have been an Officer of the Reich.

Army Tank

The bridges had all been destroyed by the French Army during their retreat in order to delay the enemies. To get across the river, there was a temporary bridge built with pieces of wood. We had to hold onto the ropes as we crossed on the narrow planks. It was right over the rapid water The German soldiers were next to me and held me at times, so I wouldn't fall. I was sobbing the entire time; I thought they were going to throw me into the river as soon as we got halfway across. I could see the raging water below us. As we walked to our house, I saw all the German flags with swastikas hanging all around us again. Hitler had visited Verdun the day before. He made it his personal vengeance to conquer our hometown, where we stopped his countrymen 20 years ago, in WWI. It was always his personal demon, he hated Verdun.

We finally made it to our house, and what a disaster it was! All the windows were broken. The doors were open, and most of the furniture was damaged. We found out later that it was the Belgian evacuees coming behind us who actually entered our homes and broke everything in sight because they were infuriated. The guard left us there.

Mom closed the door behind him, and we hugged each other, weeping silently, too proud to let the enemies know how devastated we were. Downstairs, the kitchen was not so bad, only windows were shattered. In the café section, some chairs were broken, but nothing extremely bad. We went to the second floor where the bedrooms were, and found all the furniture destroyed. The legs of the bed chopped off. It was a nightmare. On the third floor where the formal dining room was, my mom let out a scream. We ran upstairs with her and saw, the German soldiers must have just had dinner. Our expensive Limoges dishes were all dirty and the Baccarat crystal glasses still had wine and champagne in them. Empty bottles of our best wines and champagne were everywhere. Some helmets were left behind on the floor, along with those famous Germans steel curved blade boning knifes, like half-sabers.

That night, my mom let us sleep beside her on the mattress, on the floor since the legs of the bed were broken and I know she was sitting up, waiting for the invaders to come back and kill us. She said it was the longest night she had ever spent.

Early the next morning, the same guard who had carried me on the makeshift bridge came and explained in fairly decent French, "Madame, we are sorry, but when you came back so soon last night, we had barely enough time to warn the officers of your return, who were in your dining room. Someone will come during the day and retrieve everything." Seeing our apprehension, he added, "No one will harm you." I promise!

Later we heard a knock on the door, and a few soldiers in green uniforms clicked their heels, went upstairs, and picked up what the officers had left behind. At least now we were able to claim the entire house, but this didn't calm my mother's fear.

There was another knock on the door. "Madame, we have some newspapers to put in front of your windows so you can have privacy," the soldier said.

"Merci, monsieur!" she exclaimed. It was just the three of us; no one else around; no other civilian in sight.

The next day in the middle of the night, Mom woke us up. She was sitting up on the mattress where Arlette and I were sleeping. We could see fire reflecting on the building across the river. The soldiers came and banged on the door downstairs shouting, "*Achtung* (watch out)!" They escorted us to the tents they had set up for the soldiers on the Quai. Again, I was crying for water. The flames were shooting up in the sky. It seemed to me that we were surrounded by fire.

"We escaped the evacuation, but the *boches* (Germans) are going to destroy us in a fire," Mom said. "They are burning our town on purpose."

"Madame, stay in our tent, we will protect you until the fire is out," they said. They gave us water. I was shaking so badly that they took pity on us. We found out later that some officers had gotten drunk and set fire by accident to the biggest hotel in Verdun on the "Rue Mazel", the street located right behind us; in the front of The Monument de la Victoire.

When it was safe they marched us back to our house. It was such chaos with soldiers screaming and running in all directions, and we could not understand a word. How we survived this episode, I'll never know.

For the most part, they left us alone, but twice a day, someone would lift the newspaper taped on our window and leave food and water for us. We never saw the face of our rescuer; he would simply drop off supplies for us to eat and drink. So for a few days, we had relative peace in our home.

In the park across the street, Le Quai, the German troops had set up tents for the enemy soldiers to live. I don't remember how long they remained in their temporary housing. When we were growing up, we would hear so many horror stories about the enemy. To us at the time, it was as if they weren't even human; they were monsters.

I have to say that my feelings about them changed. These Germans were human and very kind, but I am only referring to the regular German Army and not the Nazis who came in later, terrorizing not only us but even their own army! During the following weeks, more and more citizens returned home.

"Bonjour Madame Petit, Josianne, Jean-Claude!" we exclaimed. We hugged and kissed each other on each cheek, as is the traditional French greeting. We were so happy we were alive and already looking into the future rather than the past.

"*Ou étiez vous* (where were you)?" we asked Josianne's mom. "We made it to Dijon, then returned here."

"We were stuck in a small town somewhere," she answered. "We are so happy to see you and that Monique made it; we kept thinking about her health."

"Oh, *voici* (here is) Madame Durand!" my mom exclaimed. "Where is your husband?"

"I don't know where they captured him, I believe he is in Germany," Madame Durand replied. "Jean Claude is now talking to Monique; he will give her the details."

It was like a holiday, having our neighbors who were like members of our own family back with us. Before the war, we hardly spoke to each other. When you own a business, social time is very limited, but now, we were all like one big family. The neighbors seemed so wonderful and caring.

Some stores started to reopen, one at a time. It took months, but we made it. We were French and proud; we were not going to let the invaders have the best of us. Now, we had a bakery, no wheat bread only corn. You take away bread from Frenchmen and we feel like we are dying, four years with rationed corn bread! The delicatessen where we could finally get some food, very little everything rationed with stamps.

For us, the bakery was one of the most important stores to reopen. It is true for French people that to lack bread is starvation itself because it is their main staple. For a few weeks, we ate French bread, but then the Germans confiscated the wheat. It was the end of our main staple for at least five years. We were eating a lot of strange bread since the grain used to make flour was in scarce supply, even non-existent. The Germans took it.

As the weeks turned into months, we had less and less food, and starvation began. It was getting to the point where my mom would give us a teaspoon of granulated corn with hot water right before we went to bed to keep the hunger away. We were given ration tickets, one pound of meat for the three of us for a month. It was the beginning of famine.

*** WWII Through the Eyes of a Child ***

Arlette and I with bank across the river in background

My first grade picture with Madame Chevalier (June 1939)

Jean Claude my best friend on the Quai de Londres

*** The True Story of Monique Raguet/Jones ***

When I was 2 years old, just before my long illness

Chapter 7: Living conditions

One of the things I remember most, especially because it scared me, was that before dark, we would have to close the shutters. My mother made black drapes and we would hang them over the windows so the light would not shine out at night. The conquering forces demanded it, and if we did not obey the rules, it would be punishable by imprisonment. The German soldiers would come and fine us or take us to jail if they saw any light shining, so we were living in constant fear.

Although the lights in our house would not be visible by putting up these black drapes and closing the shutters, it made me feel like I was in a cave, and sometimes I would have trouble breathing because of it. We had the feeling of being buried alive and were afraid of the air raids by the English and the Americans.

Electricity was scarce then. Many days, it would only be turned on for a few hours. Therefore, we would try to accomplish all the chores that required electricity within that short period of time. It was quite a task, and our lives began to revolve around those precious hours we had when the electricity was on.

During the winter, we burned briquettes of anthracite in the stove, located in the center of the café. Anthracite was a much better product than coal since it lasted longer and did not smoke. So at least we had one room that we could keep warm. My mom would ask, "*How are we going to survive?*"

We also had our stove for cooking purpose in the kitchen adjacent to the café itself. When it was extremely cold we would open the door between the two rooms.

When my mom needed errands run, she was afraid to send my attractive sister Arlette with all those soldiers in town. So since I was the youngest and the least threat to them, my job was to go and stand in line every morning in front of the creamery store. I carried a small milk can with me and bought the rationed milk for the day.

I would wait there for hours sitting on my little milk bucket, picking it up each time the line would move. My sister would tease me and call me the milk captain. I would stay there, talking to no one, making sure nobody cut in front of me. I was there every day, through the snow, the heat, and the rain. In some ways, I felt like I was training to be a milkman. From time to time, Josianne would say, "Do you want company?" I could not understand why her family did not need milk, but I was glad to have company even though I never asked her.

* * *

My grandfather and my mother decided to purchase a property outside of the city, which became our new garden.

At 5:00 in the morning, I would hear my Mom yell, "Monique, get up, it is time to go to the garden."

I was so tired, but had no choice. The garden was like paradise to me, quiet and beautiful. In the spring, we had a lot of work to do like cultivate with a shovel! I had blisters on both hands; but after that period of intense work; when the harvest time came along, it seemed like a painting from Monet, a piece of heaven. Everything growing, flowers, vegetables and fruits. It also meant food!

My grandfather lived with us for six months with us during spring and summer, then the remainder of the year with my aunt Madeleine in Nancy. The town is located in "Meurthe et Moselle" another Department. We lived in the Department of "Meuse". Nancy was only 60 miles from us.

During my Grandfather's time with us, the garden was his life and the garden was the only way we could survive starvation. I was glad when he returned to Nancy. We didn't have to be so uptight. He was so dominant, especially with me, after all I deserved some free time, but in his eyes I had to work like an adult.

First of all, our garden was located on the other side of town, so we had to walk a few miles from our café. Our garden facing the street was a hedge about eight feet tall, and on the inside was a wire fence surrounding the whole property to protect it from pests, or hungry citizens too lazy to cultivate themselves We employed a part time gardener, George, who had to stand on a ladder to trim the hedge. Maman would pay him with a bottle of wine, and he would always celebrate early. The minute he received his advance earnings.

"George had too much to drink again before he trimmed—*c'est un idiot* (he is stupid)!" said my grandfather. "Germaine, do you want to let him know, or should I tell him myself?" He is a hard worker, but the hedge is still crooked! Look at it, when he drinks he is worthless.

We would enter the gates to the garden after opening the padlocks. The scent of fresh flowers gave me a sense of entering another world with a peaceful atmosphere like a sanctuary. We had pear trees, apples, Italian prunes, three different kinds of cherries, and mirabelles (bright yellow fruits the size of cherries, very popular in the northern part of France). Their blossoms smelled so good, and their fruits like honey!

"Monique, do not walk on the plants," my grandfather would always scold me. "That's why we have grass paths between the vegetables." We had to keep the short grass cut all the time, trimming was another tedious job. It kept us from walking on the plants or dirt.

"Yes, Grandfather." (Of course was my normal answer). In order to take revenge, I would sneak some fruits without him watching me. Don't forget we were always hungry, for a child one or two strawberries, or other delicious fruits were a wonderful treat.

The grass paths were about two feet wide between the carrot patches, peas, green beans, and of course those delicious red beets. Beets were the best vegetable we could eat since they were loaded with vitamins like iron and other natural ingredients such as sugar. We had to eat them every day, so I really dislike them even to this day, please! I consumed too many. Four years on a diet of red beets would make you understand, enough is enough! Every time I see them at the market, I have flash back of the war, and our great starvation diet.

Canons

In between the rows of vegetables, we had flowers we could cut and bring to the café in bouquets. French need flowers like they need bread, or cheese! Our garden was like a miniature reproduction of the" *Garden of Versailles"* —everything was immaculate. Imagine all the different nuances, the grassy green walks, the rainbow of multiple colored flowers, the English Boxwoods with their unique aroma, the fragrant lilacs in shades of deep purple, violet and white, all different peonies, and not a weed in site. At the far end of the garden were the potato patches, and intermingled between hazelnut bushes were all kinds of berries in red, black, and white, also currants whose thorns kept intruders away. We had wire fences as a border on the other three sides without hedges. The path from the main entrance, covered with bricks, took us to a small house with windows.

"Germaine, you forgot to put the curtains up," said my grandfather. "What would you do without me?"

This house was divided in two rooms. The front had curtains, lounge chairs, a mirror, little tables with matching tablecloths, and fresh cut flowers in the vases during the season.

The other part was the working section where we stored the tools and equipment. Attached to the little house was another small building for our small animals.

Our part-time gardener/whatever, George, built cages where at least 60 rabbits were kept, and it was my responsibility to care for them. After my milk duties, I had to fetch grass every morning from the banks around us with a sickle. Do you know how many bags of grass I had to cut for so many animals? I chopped at least two burlap bags nearly as tall as I was. I had two pet rabbits, Bijou and Nicole, since their birth. I used to hold them and play with them. We would never use them for food.

Behind the house we also had hens and roosters, they would go from a patch of grass to an enclosed area through a small door where we would gather the eggs. Those chickens were so messy and noisy. Pierre the "Coq," master of his species, was nasty—beautiful yet aggressive. I was afraid of him, I can understand why the French chose the rooster for their national bird, just as America chose the eagle. Majestic animal but vicious.

Arlette would always find something to criticize me for, as a typical older sister does. "Why did you forget to bring the peonies from the garden?"

On May 1st each year, I had to cut lily of the valley and violets for my mom, which was a great French tradition. You did not dare forget!

Each product harvested was kept in my home on the Quai de Londres. In the fall, each fruit was wrapped individually and set on the third floor of the house, in our living room. The potatoes, turnips, carrots, cabbages, and beets were stored alongside of the barrels of wine in the dark basement, a cooler place. They had to last us the whole winter. We treated them as if they were gold. I transported most all of the garden products back home in a little red wagon or in the basket on my bicycle.

One day, in the afternoon, while I was coming home pulling this little wagon, an air raid alarm sounded. That meant we were all supposed to get off the streets and get to a shelter. I was on the Quai at the time, not far from my house. I started running, the vegetables were falling off the wagon, and I was making so much noise that one of the SS soldiers came out of the headquarters located a few houses from ours, and barked at me, "*Get off the street now, kid, or you won't see your parents again!*"

He turned around and I could see him smile at the other soldiers, but I was still petrified nonetheless. My sister, of course, was waiting with a grin on her face and laughed, "*You did it again — you looked like a clown!*"

When I think back on that day, I suppose she was right. I have to laugh at the noise of the wagon on the gravel with its contents flying in all directions and this little skinny thing passing the headquarters of the SS, the deadliest and most fearsome enemies. I was so innocent as a child and, determined not to lose our precious food. Fear was not part of my reasoning.

Chapter 8: Other civilian's

Another memory now comes to mind. As I was strolling to our garden, I passed a little chapel. It was the sanctuary of the nuns known as Carmelites, the same order to which St. Therese belonged. They were all dressed in long brown veils and habits. Once in a while, I would enter this sanctuary. There were gates to protect the inside of the chapel, but you could still see the nuns if you opened a little window. One day, one of the new nuns, who resembled a beautiful bride, was making her final vows, which symbolized her marriage to God. The parents of the nuns offered a great dowry to the Vatican for this occasion and made three vows: one of chastity, one of poverty, and one of silence. Therefore, if you needed to speak to them, only one nun had the privilege of communication and was able to talk to you. Like us, they had to evacuate during the war. Upon our return, it was the first time I saw some of them out of their habits and speaking to the owners of the stores in order to purchase food. They later returned to the convent and we never saw them again.

I became true pals with Jeanine Thierand, the daughter of the mayor of Verdun, because our fathers were good friends due to their positions in our community. One day she asked me, "Monique, may I go to the garden with you? I am so lonely."

"*Oui!*" I always responded. We would pick peas together and shell them, put them in a few suitcases until they were full! My parents, would take them to my aunt and uncle who owned a tobacco factory in Nancy, France.

Jeanine and I enjoyed sharing gossip. "*Monique, how does Madame Petit manage to feed Josianne and Charlie?*" she asked me. "And how did she get this new baby when her husband is a Prisoner of War in Germany?"

"*Honestly, I don't know that myself,*" I replied. "We have a really handsome client who visits the café daily whose name is Hans."

"Yes, I know who you're talking about!" Jeanine exclaimed. "He has blond hair, blue eyes, and says hello to everyone. He is very polite, unlike the rest of the troops. "I think he is an officer.

"Well," I continued, "after he visits us, he goes to see Madame Petit. I wonder why—surely he doesn't get a haircut from her every day?"

Jeanine laughed and blurted out, "I'll ask Josianne myself if you don't!"

Josianne was so nice to me that I had to personally question her about it the next time I saw her.

One day, Josianne came to my garden in tears and said, "I have to talk to someone—I don't know what is going on, but Hans is spending a lot of time with us for some reason. He even looks at my little brother as if he were his own."

"Maybe he is lonely," I replied. "Hans is so nice that he actually gave me flowers for my First Holy Communion, along with a few vegetables for us to celebrate. He was even crying because I reminded him of the little girl he lost in a bombardment."

"Really?" She said with relief.

I sensed something was wrong when I heard Josianne's comments, plus those from my parents, but I did not let her know and continued the conversation by telling her, "Hans brings us peas in a can sometimes, and we cook it for him. Did you know that he lost his whole family in Dusseldorf, Germany? They had an air raid and his wife and children were all killed. Maybe he is thinking of you as his family away from home. It is ironic because your dad is over there in a camp thinking of you."

"No one could be nicer," she said. *"Please keep this a secret, but he brings us food and milk for the baby. But, I hate those Germans."*

"But Josianne, he is different; some of them are very nice," I reassured her. *"After all, he is not a Nazi, he was drafted like your dad. He also had to leave his family and come here for his country."*

She felt better, but it was our secret and I never repeated it to Jeanine. Considering what the townspeople were gossiping about, her dad could have given her mom a lot of trouble if he found out.

Chapter 9: Trading food and transportation

The following day, my mom took me to my aunt and uncle's home. We would usually bring them some of our vegetables, and they provided my family with tobacco in return.

We, then, traded that tobacco with the local farmers for more meat and seeds for the garden. It was a very complicated matter of which I had no part because it was considered a *"grownup"* affair, as I was told many times. Getting to my aunt and uncle's was no easy task. We had to carry our passports with us at all times. As I said, we lived in Verdun, Meuse, while my aunt and uncle lived at 58 Rue de la Commanderie in Nancy, Meurthe & Moselle. The two cities are in different departments, which are the equivalent of counties or states in the United States, so transportation was very limited. It was like entering another country.

There were hardly any buses or motorcycles for civilians due to the total lack of gasoline, so we all rode our bikes whenever possible. For this reason, I actually believe that every French person is born sitting on a bike. But we had to take the bus to travel to my aunt and uncle's house, and soldiers would stop us each time we entered a new department to search us for our papers and the contents of our luggage. Whenever we met the German soldiers, we were always extremely apprehensive as to what might happen.

Were they going to kill us? Or take us prisoners?

As a result of all this work and travel outdoors during the warmer months, I began to develop quite a suntan, which was not socially acceptable, according to our social upbringing. Ladies at that time never got suntans, only farm hands did. Maman was too proud for this and would remind us we were upper-middle class citizens who did not belong in the same level as farmers. In Europe classes are very important, not like in America. Therefore, she started making me wear gloves, a large hat, and long-sleeved blouses, they were very uncomfortable in the heat.

When we traveled to my aunt's family, we would usually get dressed up to some extent. This actually worked to our advantage because the German soldiers always wanted to know if we were farmers when they stopped us at the department border, but being well dressed and lacking a suntan, we were able to claim we were not. We were visiting family. Sometimes we were fortunate to take the bus, but I always hated taking it. The fumes from the diesel fuel used to make me deadly ill. I would actually vomit the whole time. It was crammed with people and I would always get so sick!

Chapter 10: Different ways to get food

Among other things we traded, I remember that my Mother once exchanged some tobacco with a farmer for a cute and cuddly piglet. When we brought him home, we let him stay in the back of our café in the kitchen. One day when German soldiers visited our café as clients, I was told to go keep the pig silent, and close the kitchen door.

As I was holding him, he began to squeal loudly. I threw some towels over him and turned up the radio volume as high as possible, then took the pig down to the wine cellar, close the door. The Germans curiously asked what all the noise was and started searching the kitchen. My sister told them it was the radio.

They entered the kitchen and saw nothing because I had already fled to the cellar with the pig, we narrowly escaped it was a close call. We had to guard all the food we had, including the pig, rabbits, chickens, and vegetables, with our lives as we knew we could be without them at any moment. That night, we took the piglet to the butcher, who was one of our neighbors. He made sausages, pork chops, and other types of meat from every part of the animal he could possibly use. It is how we survived all those years of famine.

Chapter 11: First Holy Communion

Under our Cathedral, we discovered catacombs dated from the Roman Empire. They were found during WWI 1914-1918, when a bomb went through the church.

When I made my First Holy Communion, the café was closed, as it was during other outstanding occasions. We wore long veils, long white dresses, and gloves, which were very hot and uncomfortable, but it was one of the most important days in our young lives. I fainted right before this picture (*on page 103*) was taken due to the lack of food.

Since we were parishioners of the Cathedral and Seminary, the Mass would last at least a few hours, and at that time we could not eat after midnight before receiving communion the next day. Boring time for children. The celebration would be very solemn. It was a long day; at least 100 boys and girls participated. We had a procession from the seminary to the church. The Bishop, being the head of our cathedral, was the main officiating priest. The clergy joined us also.

Our neighbors helped us celebrate the occasion by giving us special French dishes, and our German friend even brought some too.

The Germans did not bother us that day. Except for Charlie, the German officer who brought me the flowers.

My First Holy Communion,
June 21, 1942

The replica of St. Peter's altar

The Cathedral of Verdun with the red-roofed
seminary attached to its basilica

For dessert, we had a special treat that Mom purchased at the bakery on the Rue Mazel. Because we lived in Verdun, the bakery had patented a large chunk of chocolate that resembled a bomb airplanes would drop during WWI and WWII.

It was made of thick dark chocolate with a wick going through the center. When you lit the wick, the bomb would explode and all sorts of French candies flew all over the room. Verdun is known for this specialty or *"chef d'oeuvre"* (work of art).

The crypt of the Cathedral of Verdun basilica

Chapter 12: The German occupation

The German soldiers marched frequently in steps called *"Le Pas de Parade."*, picture shown *(on page 34)*. They would lift one leg at a time up to their waists and clicked their shining leather boots whenever they stopped or saluted. What an awful sound they made. They also wore those very large steel plates in front of their uniforms that I had I mentioned. After a year or more, the SS regiment, the most feared army, came to Verdun and everything changed. Their Headquarters were established just a few doors down from us on the same street. There was a distinct difference between the two German armies. The regular army wore green uniforms, while the other had black uniforms with the letters SS embroidered in red on their vests, coats, and hats. They petrified all of us, even the other Germans who were mobilized for the war, and were not volunteers.

"Arlette," Mom said, "here come a bunch of *boches*; make sure you keep the good whiskey and the *Chateau Neuf du Pape* wine hidden. They can drink beer."

"Can I go upstairs to learn my German?"

"I don't know why you have to learn it" she would ask. "I hate to be with the soldiers and the smell of their continuous cigarette smoking."

"German in school," my mother murmured under her breath. "I forbid you to speak that language in front in me!"

"I have to," I replied. "You know, we have to do what they want. My next language will be English."

Arlette added, "At least she was able to learn Latin first."

We had to learn the old writing, which was extremely difficult. Now, you can only find it in the records of old Protestant Churches.

Every Saturday evening, we were treated to classical music on the Quai in the front of our house. The German Army had the best classical bands. That was when I began to appreciate classical music. I remember one of those nights, when my father returned home — we had a wonderful time.

Many of the fathers who were mobilized or recalled to the French army had returned. It was after the Government of Vichy took place, when half of France was occupied while the other was not. Maréchal Petain, the hero of WWI, helped to restore the government. He was 100% French, a real politician and an expert at keeping both sides calm.

Pierre Laval, head of the National Assembly, was really a traitor, he suggested that Maréchal Petain become President of the council for *l'État Français (the French state)* during this time, he was a puppet president. All of France knew Petain's hands were tied, but at least he stopped the enemies from invading the entire country. At least we had someone we could put our trust in, even if we knew he could not save us. He represented a little light of hope.

Chapter 13: Close call for my Mother

One day, the SS knocked on our door and told Mom they would execute her within 24 hours if she did not get rid of the pigeons we still had in the attic. They kept flying back to their nests. My Mom had to go up to the attic and kill all of the wonderful pigeons; descendants of their warriors ancestors it was truly a sad day. They were the reason my Father received the "Legion of Honneur" from our president. (*Picture page 40*).

That is the only time she did not allow me to go with her in the attic. Pigeons were considered a threat to the invaders since they were used for sending notes or signals to people, during the First War. They were considered a weapon against the Germans. Which is why they were going to arrest us. They thought we may be part of the underground.

When the **SS** (Special Service, devoted to Hitler); arrived, some of our neighbors were forced to wear gold Stars of David *(Picture page 131)* on their clothes, like I wore my name tag during the evacuation. I didn't know what it meant at the time, but anyone wearing these stars would eventually be taken away during the night and never returned. I remember hearing my parents crying, early the following morning, but I was too young to understand what was going on or for my parents to explain it to me.

Life changed, even the regular German army became very cautious of them. They were our real enemies!

"Josianne, what's going on?" I asked her. "Did Hans, who was not an SS, tell your mom why Mr. & Mrs. Rosenthal left during the night? My mother says their business will be closed for a while."

"I don't know," she replied, "I also heard Hans was going to the Russian Front. My mom is in tears continuously. What a coincidence; we were told my dad is coming back soon."

In the meantime my father came back from the south of France, he was not captured due to the dividing line we had. The enemies stopped invading the south of France at the town of Vichy, with the fake French Government.

For two years, I had wondered why the only men in Verdun operating businesses were Italians.

"They are our enemies," Arlette answered bitterly. "They do not have to fight! Their stores prospered while our Frenchmen were away, I always wondered why."

After all, it was the Italians who tried to ambush us while we were on the train, disguised as Priests and Nuns, and dive-bomb us in several occasions, while we were walking along the road during the evacuation!

Now, that we were home, I somehow contracted lice, which was considered shameful in those days, and I had to go through the agony of my parents combing my hair with a fine-toothed comb twice a day, applying powder, and wearing a black cape. For a while, I could not go to school.

Germans in particular don't believe in poor health. If I walked out in public, I thought they were shunning me. My Mother was so disgraced that I had contracted lice in school. Yet I had never caught them during the entire evacuation despite sleeping in hay and grass. Among all sorts of people not able to wash, dirty, and so were we, all the refugees. I had really long blond hair, my Mom was very careful with it. My sister with her brown hair was not as much in danger of catching those pests.

Chapter: 14 Prisoners of War coming home

When Josianne's Dad came home, the neighbors made sure to tell him about the new baby. However, Mr. Petit was a real gentleman and told the nosy neighbors,
"I forgive my wife. I am not blind; I know about the baby. They had to survive during the war. Who are you to judge her? It is my personal problem, not yours."

He understood the reason for his wife's actions. The family came first, and she was not a bad wife, but a good mother. She simply wanted to prevent her children from starvation. Charlie, her other son, had developed a very large stomach, so of course, I was curious why.

"What's wrong with him?" I asked.

"When you get hungry, the air in your stomach blows it up," she explained.

Madame Petit was not privileged like we were and had no other way out. Hans vanished, I supposed to the Russian Front. We never heard from him after that.

113

Yes, another time, I asked my mother an embarrassing question, "Mom, why do those made-up girls go past our place every Wednesday morning?"

"Monique, you are always asking questions. They are 'ladies of the night.' The forces of occupation use them. You will understand as you get older. They go to a doctor to make sure they are in perfect health. Soldiers need companionship when they are away from home."

"*Where do they live?*" I persisted.

"They live behind the cement wall topped with broken glass, the one you pass when you go take the sheets to get washed and ironed at the Laundromat."

The Laundromat was like a factory. I would drop the sheets off, in my famous little red wagon, one day and pick them up the next when they were finished, similar to a dry cleaning service.

"Ah," I answered, without the slightest idea of what she just explained, except I knew the place she was talking about.

Chapter: 15 Feeling about Germans

Everybody around us knew how I loathed the Germans. Even after we heard the saying "they have an air of thoroughbred horses" and they were extremely cultured, they were our enemies nevertheless.

When you grow up in a region beside the enemy's border, you learn to hate those strangers just because your parents told you to. I would do whatever a child could do to show rebellion because I was a purebred Frenchwoman, and brainwashed by my surrounding. My skin would crawl when they would all stand up in the café and sing the German national anthem out loud. What a slap in the face it was.

"Hey, Monique, did you stand at attention last *night when the* "*Fritz*" (another derogatory name for Germans) *were singing?"* asked Jean Claude, smiling from ear to ear.

"No, I turned up the radio as loud as I could instead. I hate when they sing"

Mixed weapon turret

Anti-tank rails within the
Maginot Line

Part of the Parade (*rest on page 46*)

St. Cyr Cadets

*** The True Story of Monique Raguet/Jones ***

THE STARS AND STRIPES
Daily Newspaper of U.S. Armed Forces — in the European Theater of Operations

Vol. 4 No. 260   New York, N.Y.—London, England—France   Saturday, Sept. 2, 1944

Verdun Falls; Meuse Crossed

Reds Drive 10 Mi. Past Bucharest

Reach Bulgarian Border; Nazi Offensive Near Warsaw Peters Out

With all Rumania's main strategic points now in Russian hands Soviet tanks and motorized infantry thrust on swiftly beyond captured Bucharest yesterday in a lightly-opposed advance that promised a quick link-up with Tito's Jugoslav Partisans and conquest of the whole Danube Valley as far as the "Iron Gate" 100 miles east of Belgrade.

Spearheads of Gen. Rodion Malinovsky's army had pushed ten miles southwest of the Rumanian capital within a few hours of its fall and other units reached the Bulgarian border in the neighborhood of the Danube port of Giurgiu, 36 miles south of Bucharest.

Berlin reported "major battles" north of fallen Ploesti, where Malinovsky launched a secondary thrust to penetrate the Carpathians into Transylvania and

His Heritage

Yanks Sweeping On; British, Canadians Seize Arras, Dieppe

Across the last war's bloody battlegrounds, through the mighty fortress of Verdun into St. Mihiel and over the River Meuse, Gen. Patton's Third Army smashed ahead yesterday on the last 50 miles to the border of Germany.

And their Allies on their left flank rolled in high gear up the flying-bomb area at a mile-an-hour clip. The British pushed well into the Pas de Calais inland from the coast and reached Arras, 28 miles from the Belgian border, after pushing forward better than 30 miles from Amiens in 24 hours. The Canadians, without firing a shot, captured Dieppe, where the commando raid of two years ago cost them so dearly.

It was the fifth anniversary of the day Hitler started the war with his attack on Poland, and it found the Allies farther east at some points, the United Press said, than the line the Germans held when they asked for the armistice in 1918; the particular points were not specified.

Along the whole 130-mile arc of the U.S. 12th Army Group, the Yanks thrust forward during the day an average of more than 20 miles. The Nazis' blitzkrieg to Paris looked impressive in 1940—but the Americans were covering the same ground in the other direction in just half the time.

From Verdun, according to German Radio, the Yanks drove into the Lorraine basin, which presumably means the big coal and iron industry area in this region. The radio said American forces established three bridgeheads across the

B26s Pummel Nazis at Brest

118

Chapter 16: Air Raids

We had air raids all the time. The sirens would scream loudly and terrify us day and night. We had become so accustomed to our routine when we heard the sirens that we became like robots. We would automatically run back to our house, where we kept our clothes on a chair beside our bed, and hide in the cellar.

If we had time we would run to "The Monument de la Victoire" our air raid shelter with our gas mask. During the night, we would have our clothes ready on a chair beside the bed. We knew exactly where every piece of clothing was, and the gas mask, even in the dark. We only possessed so many minutes to run one block to the air raid shelter or down the cellar.

The Allied bombardiers set sites and released bombs on little French villages, sometimes destroying them, and sacrificing hundreds of lives for what seemed to us to be no apparent reason and totally uncalled for.

I was told later on it was due to the extra amount of bombs they carried and the danger of the planes exploding in the air or during landing outweighed sparing the few villages. I supposed it was as good an explanation as we could get. It does not seem fair to me, to kill so many innocent people to safe one or two pilots! But War does not make sense.

My parents told me that Verdun was safe since we were the parent city of London, England. My street was named after London (Quai de Londres) for that reason.

I always believed that theory, it helped mentally.

At last, we began returning to school, located on top of a hill behind the *Monument de la Victoire*, and we would have air raid drills at least once a day. Every morning, we practiced running down 350 steps from the top of the "Monument de la Victoire" from my school to the shelter, down below. *(Picture page 30)*. While running down the steps of the monument, we had to secure a gas mask from the back of the student preceding us and get to the shelter beneath the monument, all within **three minutes**. We were timed since it meant life or death in the case of a real bombardment. We did it over and over again until we became pros. I still remember looking through the goggles of the mask while running down the stairs.

I still cannot stand wearing anything on my face such as goggles for skiing or swimming, and I have a hard time catching my breath it scares me so. Actually, it took me many years to figure out why I could not tolerate things on my face, until I realized it was due to this horrible memory.

The Germans were very keen on us exercising consistently. It was their major goal not only in France but even in their own country and all occupied territories to practice healthy habits. The first thing we did in the morning when we entered my school was get out our mats, put them on the floor, and exercise.

Jeanine would tease me, "Hey, Monique, I wish Jean Claude could see you now — you are such an athlete!"

"Be quiet!" I would answer laughing and I couldn't even go across the beam without falling.

We exercised intensely for one hour each day. Germans are very athletic and constantly trying to improve their health. Looking back, I now realize they were training us for more sinister purposes: they wanted us to be healthy specimens in order to be recruited for Hitler's ideal generation. The exercises we did in school did have a positive side. In fact, I've been working out every day since then and it has become a major part of my life.

We had to learn how to swim, but it was not a popular sport in my region. I nearly drowned during these training sessions. They would attach some sort of harness that hooked from the ceiling and then dangle us in the water. Some girls would say they couldn't swim because it was that time of the month. I was too young to know what they meant, so I gave the same excuse every week, which worked for a while until the guards caught on and asked me, "Kid, how could it be the wrong time every Tuesday?"

Since I had no idea what these girls were talking about, the excuse was not good enough and they made me get in the water anyway. It was very hard to learn to swim, but I did nonetheless. They had to rescue me from drowning because the belt was not tight enough and I sank to the bottom of the pool.

I fell head first from the supporting belt. According to the other students, they pulled me out from the side and revived me. It took me another 30 years to finally learn to swim. I could not even get in the water at first. I decided to overcome this fear when two of my children became lifeguards later in life and I was embarrassed about my lack of swimming abilities.

The scariest memory for me was when they would put us through tests in order to measure the air capacity in our lungs . Every Saturday we would have to breathe into a machine, which would then measure the air contained in our lungs. Now considering I was very skinny, the Germans were afraid I would contract tuberculosis. Therefore, I worried from week to week about the nightmare test. Children who did not make it were sent to a sanatorium. It was a terrifying experience every time because we never knew what would happen if we failed.

I often wondered, *"Would I be able to go back home? Would they send me away? Would we ever see our family again?"* I had to endure that throughout the duration of the German occupation.

Under the strict order of the German army, the teachers gave us cookies for our afternoon break during school. These weren't cookies that were full of sugar and tasted pleasant, but were actually small cakes designed to give us vitamins and ingredients we were missing from our diet. They tasted awful, but we were so hungry that we didn't care. I think the Germans referred to them as cookies so we would feel better about eating them.

"Jeanine, I didn't see you chewing your food this morning," I observed once. "What did you do with the stuff they gave us?"

She looked around her, making sure no one could hear her and said, "It's in my pocket!"

I was so surprised since the authorities watched us while we were consuming them, so I just had to ask, "How did you manage that one?"

Jeanine said with a smile, "Do you remember when Jean Claude was coughing so loud? No one was watching!"

"You are so mischievous," I replied, "but considering we have no idea what exactly we're eating, it's scary."

"I forgot to tell you, my dad heard from the German officials that we would not have class for two days next week," Jeanine added. "It is confidential, so keep quiet, or else I'll get in trouble."

"Why?" I said. "What's going on?"

"They want to vaccinate us at school because they do not want us to carry diseases," she responded.

Sure enough, we were all inoculated for various illnesses. All blond hair and blue eyes children, lined up in the corridors, then the SS soldiers closed the doors and gave us our shots. Again, some of us were scared and screaming. Other kids even fainted. We never knew what they injected us with. In some ways I felt like we were guinea pigs for something or other. But for me, whatever those shots contained evidently helped me, because my illness never came back and I have been very healthy since then. At least some good has come out of this. I also believed that God was with us and helped us.

Hitler was always trying to build an elite group of humans. He was consumed by this. I happened to have the qualifications.

We would need to get dressed up to witness the German parades, so I had to get my best dress and make sure I looked fine.

Jeanine, Josianne and Jean Claude all said to me giggling "We dare you to wear your blue, white and red dress!"

"Watch me, I will!" I replied defiantly. "I hate those *boches* — I am French!"
Without the Germans realizing, I put on a white outfit with some red and blue, the French colors. I would go and watch the parades in that dress. I couldn't believe that I was never stopped. Part of me feels it may have been because I was so skinny and pitiful looking that they never bothered even looking at me.

Another time, my friends tried to stop me from running past the German guards and jumping over the rifles stacked against each other in the shape of a pyramid, just to irritate the French population.

The regular troops were not very harmful and played with us, and it was a distraction we provided them with. It was worth it because I did not get in trouble. Instead, I gained respect from my classmates. It wasn't all that bad and thinking back, it was my sister and her friends who edged me on to do daring little things like that to take advantage of my youth. They were typical teenagers, and I later found out they belonged to the FFL (French underground), except my sister.

The city of Verdun, being so despised by Germans because of their defeat during the first War in 1914-1918, it was a place where French, German, and other foreign diplomats visited, along with kings, queens, and many important diplomats. They came mainly to the cemeteries.

Most of the High German dignitaries also paraded there. Among them, I saw Generals Rommel, Rundstedt, Goering, Hess, Franz Von Papen, Ribbentrop and many more high-ranking officers proudly reviewing their troops. While we watched the overwhelming pageantry and the planes fly by, the enemy tanks made us extremely sad and depressed when they passed by. Was this our new life to become Germans? Would we ever be free again?

A lot of the French soldiers were prisoners of war in Germany. They worked in the factories. My neighbor's husband was one of them. We found out later they were helping France by sabotaging numerous things constructed in Germany, such as bombs and ammunitions.

Arlette called me into the kitchen one day in tears while Mom was not home. "Monique, I need your help. I am very fond of a German officer from Munich, Germany. He was Hans' best friend. Do you remember him? He looked like the movie star Nelson Edie, who played in a few movies with Jeannette McDonald."

"No, you take care of the café, I do the rest, remember? I do not worry about your personal affairs," I responded. She was always mistreating me since I was younger.

My sister pleaded, "I am sorry, I have been too severe with you. I work very hard myself, you know."

"What were you doing talking to him? If mom finds out, she is going to kill you!" I said.

"I know, but he was so nice. He even gave us ration tickets and you and mom didn't even know about it.

During four years we had ration tickets to eat.

Besides, he is Austrian, not German. He told me he would return after the war to marry me. He is so handsome and polite, still single, and was a professor at the University of Munich before the war. Look, he gave me this beautiful Edelweiss flower (*see picture page 131*). He had to risk his life to pick it on the top of the mountains in the Alps," she persisted.

"I don't care! You never talk to me, except when you want me to do your dirty work. What do you want now?" I snapped.

"He just went to the front line a few days ago and gave me his address. He will write to me through the Red Cross," she said.

"So?" I remarked.

"Well, Mademoiselle Gigi, the maid at the hotel near us, received a letter from him. Would you please get it for me?" she begged.

So I had to sneak out and go to the hotel to find Gigi and get the letter. How on earth did she socialize with Gigi in the first place?

The next day Arlette told me, "Monique, I will give you your favorite candies if you take this letter to the post office."

Star of David badge

Edelweiss flower

Chapter 17: The Liberation

We used to listen to the BBC, the British Broadcasting Company, because they would play different types of music and would give us a chance to find out what was going on with the war. I particularly liked Beethoven's Fifth Symphony, which meant the beginning of an important announcement.

Sometimes it sounded like crickets were in the box or a lot of static. The German Wehrmacht did not want us to hear the latest news regarding the war. When we heard the first few beats of the symphony, we dropped whatever we were doing. We were glued to the radio and hoped German soldiers would not visit our café at that moment.

Arlette's school friends had since joined the French underground (FFL, *Forces Françaises Libres*). They were nearly a generation older than I was, and so we had little in common. Of course, they never found out about my sister's secret crush on one of their enemies.

"Monique, we're a lot friendlier now," I am going to tell you a secret. Then Arlette explained. "The guys [her FFL friends] told me something big is going to happen very soon. They heard the news from the BBC."

On June 6, 1944, my parents were whispering and smiling, as if keeping a big secret. We were all looking at each other and in a good mood for once. While no one talked, I could see grins on their tired and haggard faces. I knew something was going on. I didn't know it was the American and British invasion of Normandy. We, of course, didn't hear any of the details until after the Germans left us.

Meanwhile, the SS commander seemed extremely agitated and nasty. Another Jewish business owner was awakened during the night. We heard crying and protesting, but I was not told what happened.

By August, we received more news. We learned that General Leclerc and General Charles De Gaulle were helping the Allied troops. Leclerc was our personal favorite because he came from Lorraine, my province, and his emblem was the Lorraine Cross, (*Picture page 14*) which was a symbol of our region of France and of Joan of Arc. On August 31, our underground friend, Fernand Legay, told my sister in secret to get out of town and go to our outside villa as soon as possible.

"Pretend you are going to your garden and have Monique take her little red wagon," he said.

"*Why?*" Arlette asked.

"*I can't tell you; please do as I ask,*" he replied.

So we spread the word to a few neighbors and pretended to go to our garden. We heard rifles, machine guns, bombs, and V2s being fired. The V2s were scarier than the bombs because they sounded like tin cans and randomly fell anywhere; three hundred of them were launched by the German Wehrmacht still in the stage of being testing. We had experienced them in the past a few times. Hearing one passing above you meant probable death. It was the beginning of the missiles at NASA. Who knew at the time?

During the fighting that day, our neighbor who lived next to our garden had a more solid house, so they asked us to join them in their basement. I thought this would be my last day on earth. While we were down in the cellar, we heard a lot of Germans shouting and running past the house, along with more gunfire and tanks rolling by.

Suddenly, it was quiet and we heard church bells starting to ring. We were liberated!!!!!

We went outside, and to our surprise, we had survived the occupation. The roaring of tanks going through the fields behind our garden was not the Germans but Americans. It was the First American Army, Seventh Division. We stood there, frozen in time in front of the house, and couldn't believe what we saw. The Germans were still present, but they were running. So we went back inside to hide while we waited for them to leave.

The bells meant Verdun was liberated, but we were just outside of town, and the fighting was still very real. Would a desperate German soldier try to get in and shoot us all?

We then saw bright pink tanks chasing the Panzer Army. We could not understand why Americans used those bright colors instead of camouflage. We later learned that due to the rapidity of them chasing the enemy, the American airplanes had trouble distinguishing the enemies from their own army, so they attached fluorescent pink plastic tarps to the hoods of the tanks.

I remember Fernand Legay told my sister that he would cut the wires attached to the dynamite the Germans had placed beneath "Le Pont Poincare" bridge in case they had to leave Verdun in a hurry like they did in previous towns and blew them up. It was the infamous plank bridge I walked across when we returned from the evacuation four years ago and was located on the main road going through Verdun toward Germany. It had been restored a few months after the German invasion.

Verdun is surrounded by water, bridges are the only way in or out of the city. When we returned home, we learned that Fernand had indeed crawled under the bridge and cut the wires just as the last German soldier was lighting up the fuses and leaving. The enemies wanted to delay the American troops, but due to Fernand's heroism, the explosion did not occur! What a hero he became as a result of this unselfish act.

When we arrived in town, there were a bunch of men playing bagpipes in plaid skirts called kilts, as we soon learned. We had never seen Scotsmen before, so "different-looking" was an understatement. We were quite amazed at this display; the whole scene was new to our culture. Some of the American soldiers were trying to march in line when entering town, but they were too exhausted and looked a bit disheveled, yet they were still smiling, after they went through!

We were disappointed because we were expecting the French army, but nevertheless, we were deliriously happy and grateful. Such a feeling cannot be put into words.

When the tanks rolled in, we were told they were General Patton's troops. His tactic in time of war was to put a tank in each corner of the city. Since our house was located in the corner of Le Quai de Londres and La Rue Edmund Robin, a tank was located on our sidewalk, on each side. The Quai was filled with numerous tanks. We all celebrated—what a day that was. Young teenagers climbed on top of the those awful machines to kiss the soldiers, who in turn gave them candy bars and stockings.

"Monique, look at Josianne up there kissing the American soldiers just like her mother did," mom commented. *"I forbid you to move from the house!"*

My mom kept the café closed and locked for quite a few months. We learned the day after the Allies' successful liberation of our city that the French underground had shaved the heads of the women who had associated with the Germans. It became a vendetta. People were at each other's throats for befriending with the enemy. The French paraded the collaborators through the main streets and spit on them as they walked by. It was a horrible sight that reminded me of Jesus as he was on his way to the cross while his former friends spit on him.

It was just unforgettable how some people wanted revenge. We were scared, so once again, we locked our doors and windows immediately. Arlette kept looking at me and trembling until my mom asked her why. She finally had to confess her feelings toward the German officer. At this point, my mother lost her temper and physically attacked my poor sister. It was a nightmare, and we did not know if Gigi would say something. After a while, when my mom settled down, the three of us huddled together and we did not speak until the situation was over.

On September 1, 1944, three days after the troops were in France and our city was liberated, mom told dad, "Jean, I just saw three red balls descending from the sky above the bank on the other side of the river!"

"Germaine, they are flares — the **_boches_** are back!" he screamed.

We knew how much Hitler hated Verdun and was therefore coming back to destroy us. We came downstairs and hid under the sink constructed of solid granite then moved down into the cellar. We heard the tanks firing their machine guns. Since the tanks were located on our side walks, they were extremely loud and shook the whole building. I was trying to get out of the cellar to run to the air raid shelter on the Rue Mazel, one block away from us, three times I attempted to climb the steps, and three was thrown back because the house was vibrating so badly from all the shooting. I started screaming.

Suddenly, an American soldier opened the door of our cellar and appeared at the top of the steps, then helped my family and I escape. Somehow this heroic soldier heard our cries even though our doors were locked. He found a ladder and climbed up through a window on the first floor to save us, then helped us run to the shelter and made sure we got to safety. As Arlette was crossing the road (the Rue Mazel, where our "bunker," the Monument de la Victoire was), she was struck with wires from electric poles that were shattered from the bombs and hanging overhead. They tangled all over her body and we feared she would be electrocuted, but fortunately, the electricity was off. The impact from the explosions was so intense that I got blown across the street into the air and ended up inside the shelter with the rest of the people. I was later told it was like a Mary Poppins story. I suppose my body was so light that it did not take much to pick me up and send me airborne. Of course, the first thing I said was, "I am so thirsty. I want my mom, where are dad and Arlette?"

We spent the night there in safety. We later heard that over **800 bombs** were dropped over Verdun. One of the bombs was buried on the sidewalk right outside our door, just ten feet from our house. It was a miracle that only a few of them exploded in the whole town. Apparently, the French prisoners of war had sabotaged them when they were working on these explosives in the war plants in Germany. During that night in the air raid refuge, one of my neighbors gave birth to a little girl. We were all praying for the child.

We walked back to our house the next morning, extremely apprehensive. We fixed the shattered glass and picked up all the fallen statues and chairs and reset them on the floor. Some of them were broken, but others were saved. The two bronze statues (*photo on page 28*) on the marble fireplace that I used to see all the time when I was ill had fallen to the floor. The bottom of one of the statues was cracked and still bears the marks of war. They are so precious to me that I brought them with me to the United States, where they are in a place of honor in our home. They are my most prized possessions.

In the following days, big black dirigible ships, also known as barrage balloons, invaded the skies. They had enormous nets attached from one to the other. They were positioned high enough in the sky to stop low aircrafts from coming back to our city. The whole American army positioned tanks and jeeps all over town. Military police were stationed on each corner to direct traffic and make sure the roads where cleared. The MP's (Military Police) were perched on small stands and wore white gloves, helmets, belts, guns on their sides, and whistles in their mouths they used them loudly and continuously. We had a curfew at 5 p.m. and as soon as dusk fell, we would hear gunshots and machine guns being fired from one side of the river Meuse to the other side. We would lie horrified on the floor. It was no longer the enemies terrorizing our town, but actually American soldiers, convicted felons, released from the prisons in Louisiana who had the choice of fighting overseas or going back to jail. It was one battalion against another. They were criminals back home and terrorized not only civilians, but anyone who was in their way. The MPs would chase the convicts who had committed rape or theft through the towns, where they tried to escape by jumping from roof to roof. They would then break glass and jump through windows in the attics (*mansards is the French word*) of French houses. We had to barricade our doors, lock up our windows, and put wooden boards across them from side to side. The café was closed until the Battle of Bastogne was over. It took one full year. What a huge disgrace to all the soldiers who had fought so hard in the Seventh Division and Patton's army to now. Those criminals wearing the allied uniform being chased around town while wearing them. It was not the way we had pictured our Heroes, whom we had waited four long years. I guess things like this can happen during wartime. Young men leaving their home, loose in a foreign country, armed, being able to drink, feeling like Gods.

The troops moved through the country of Lorraine quickly. The commanders were able to round up the escaped convicts in less than two months. Now the criminals were under control and incorporated into the regular army.

During this time, I had my first taste of a donut through the American Red Cross, and we were also treated to wonderful concerts from well known big bands directed by famous people like Tommy Dorsey, Harry James, Benny Goodman, and others. It was a totally new sound to us—no more classical, but dance music instead. I was not allowed to go to dances because my mom thought it was not respectable enough for her family. She was right; only "loose" girls attended them.

"Monique," Josianne asked one day, "do you want to come to the dance with me? A bunch of us girls are going."

"Are the mothers going to chaperone you?" I asked in reply.

"No, we are old enough!" she said.

"Sorry Josianne, I can't go, but I will be listening to the music from home; we can hear it on the Quai," I responded.

"You are such chickens; nothing is good enough for you and Arlette," she snapped.

We started to see signs forbidding us to cross the streets that were posted along the main artery in Verdun and the surrounding area, including The Poincare Bridge and the road that passed our garden. We soon discovered why. There were tanker trucks delivering gas to the front line, known as The <u>Red Ball Express</u>. This special convoy was driven by a regiment consisting solely of black troops. Americans were moving so fast that they were running out of fuel.

They took priority and no questions were asked; we all made sure the way was cleared. When the soldiers would stop or slow down near our garden, we would give them fresh tomatoes and fruits. They in turn would give us Hershey bars or cans of Spam. We were still so hungry that Spam was the best thing of all, to us. Sometimes they would even give us silk stockings, which were in great demand at that time. Arlette would simulate stockings by first applying a coat of tan makeup from a large bottle and drawing a line up the back of her legs with a black pen. It was the style at that time.

"*Monique, don't bump me, quit it!*" Arlette would yell.

"I didn't mean to, but it serves you right for always telling on me!" I would laugh under my breath. If I was upset with her, I would happen to do that "by accident." It was my little prank to get even; or show her the picture with the enormous bow on her head at my Grandma's house. (*picture page 12*).

Another one of my numerous jobs was to go to the store where stockings were repaired and wait for hours until the lady would crochet the fine silk back into them. Receiving a pair of silk stockings from a soldier was a great gift. It was impossible to purchase them, even if you had money.

Around Christmas, we heard the Germans were returning. Hitler had surrounded the Americans in Bastogne in the Argonne country in Belgium, about 50 miles away and was marching toward Verdun again. We would hear the rattling of the guns when we pressed our ears to the ground, and we knew the fighting was growing closer. Many heroic Allied soldiers lost their lives in the battle of Bastogne.

The sirens sounded off for several nights, and we would get dressed without speaking to each other and run as fast as we could to our shelter. The tracer bullets from the tanks and the searchlights trying to catch the planes would all light up the sky. It was a horrible Christmas Night. Lights advertising new store openings remind me of those moments of sheer terror.

In the meantime, the whole town would have to go to la Citadelle, the shelter located at the other end of town, every evening. (*Picture on page 35*) We stayed down there all night. The shelter was built in the Roman Era. From the entrance were different corridors going in all directions into chambers. Upon entering they were other hallways leading somewhere else. It was an underground city used for centuries. During WWI, the French army utilized this larger-than-life fort.

The Monument of Bastogne

We received orders from the mayor after those violent nights to leave our homes every evening. The whole town had a 5 p.m. curfew and we all had to be there in the front of the main gate (*see picture page 35*). Each family would bring a pillow and a blanket and find a place to sleep down there on the ground. There were dozens of rats. I even gave names to some of them. My mom, of course, would not sleep and stayed vigilant. She feared some of the people there even more than the rats. Old, young, children, drunks, and all types had to be bunched together like we were during the evacuation.

One day when we were all in place at the time of the curfew, Mom suddenly cried, "Here we go again, the *boches* are coming back to kill us!"

The sky blackened with German planes diving toward the entrance, and men and women were screaming all bunched up, "Open the gate, open the gate! For Heaven's sake!"

No one opened the main entrance, and we were positive we were all going to be massacred.

The panic was so bad that I saw grown men trying to climb the walls, at least 10 stories high! My mom dove on top of my sister and me to protect us. There was screaming and crying everywhere; it was utter chaos. We were trapped with the guns of the *Luftwaffe* airplanes swooping toward the crowd. The buzzing of the bullets above us was just like the evacuation when we were shelled by Italian planes, our enemies at that time. I really do not know how many casualties we had, but Arlette kept pointing them to us, it was at least a few dozen.

We believe the person who forgot to open the door (in purpose) was a German sympathizer and it was his duty to let us get slaughtered at this place surrounded by stone walls. We had nowhere to go. A lot of people got killed around us, but Hitler was unable to eliminate the population of Verdun, one more time, he failed It was another nightmare we endured. Finally the American planes counterattacked and drove the Germans away.

The paratroopers returning from the front line of the Battle of Bastogne, would sell their parachutes. The material was beautiful, high quality white silk. We would purchase them and have our dressmaker sew blouses and dresses for my family out of the ones we could not sell to others. Material was extremely scarce, almost even null, but we were able to purchase wool and knit sweaters in different colors. Every six months, we took them apart and re-knitted other pullovers in different colors and shapes, with the same wool. They looked like brand new items.

I should mention something about my Father, when I first saw him wearing his captain uniform; he looked so perfect to me, strong, powerful. He was recalled as I said to command a French battalion in the South of France. He did not return to Verdun for a few years. He was afraid to put his family in danger. His underground involvement plus the possession of some tenuous pigeons who kept coming back to their home 39 Quai de Londres as I said previously, the punishment would be death, not only for him but also for his family. Upon his return, like many other Frenchmen who were not prisoners of War, he went back to his original assignment as Postmaster of Verdun.

Hand grenade

My dad had owned a garden on his old property; he did not spend of lot of time in it. He grew tobacco; sweet potatoes, lima beans, hot peppers, and vegetables he was used to eating in his native southern part of France. He had a different attitude from my Mom and Grandfather whose garden was immaculate. Food was not as important to him; my mom was very concerned about feeding us. My mother and grandpa used to refer to it as an herbal patch because it was so full of weeds. I used to enjoy going to the garden with him all the time. I didn't have to work there. One day, I came across an odd-looking object in his garden and brought it to my dad.

"Dad, look at the strange potato I found!" I said.

It turns out the "potato" was a live grenade from WWI. I am fortunate it did not detonate in my hands; I could have lost my life. My father immediately discarded it, threw it as far as he could, and it exploded. My mom forbade me to go to my dad's garden without her, when she found out about this.

Many persons do not realize how many live grenades from past wars are still scattered about people's properties. For this reason, the late Princess Diana from England had made it her mission to rid third-world countries of grenades and land mines.

My father was promoted to a higher position, as the Head Postmaster of our Department of Meuse, in Bar le Duc, which is the capital. He left us again. My mom did not want to jump too fast and decided to stay in Verdun for a while.

*** The True Story of Monique Raguet/Jones ***

We went to my dad's new apartment just before we had to evacuate Verdun again. The French authorities were afraid the German were going to invade our town again, they were so near! I was so frightened that my mother, sister, and I stayed at his place until after the American troops won the horrible battle of Bastogne. Many heroic soldiers from the 101st Airborne Division were killed, some of which were no older than sixteen years. Even though the weather was against them, they fought to the end. American General McAuliffe refused to surrender and famously answered "Nuts!" to the Germans. The Americans won , we came back home again.

We returned to our home in Verdun, and our café finally reopened. One of my friends, Robert Rati, was a sixteen-year-old paratrooper there, as I eventually found out. When the Americans returned to France, he was part of the 101st Airborne Division in the Battle of Bastogne. He was a hero in Verdun prior to his act of patriotism. When his parents' farm caught on fire, he entered the barn and saved all the horses and cattle.

He then joined the American troops by pretending he was older. I met him one day in my mom's café while I was trying to translate English into French, which I had just learned in College. All of a sudden, this young soldier said to me, "Mademoiselle, your English is very good, but you missed this and that."

I was mortified. His French was so good. "How do you speak French so well?" I asked him. "Why did you let me make a fool of myself?"

"*Je m'appelle* (my name is) Robert Rati," he said with a big grin on his face. "I have known you for many years; my parents came to your café many times."

"I didn't recognize you; you've changed so much. Did you join the Army?" I asked.

"Yes, I just came back from Bastogne, I was in the 101st Airborne Division," he replied.

My mom was listening and said to me, "Monique, he is the boy who was in the papers a few years ago for saving the livestock on his farm. Welcome home, Robert, we hope to see you often now. Maybe you could tutor Monique with her English and get reacquainted."

It was the beginning of my first romance.

"Robert, what are you going to do now?" I asked.

Robert answered me with a serious look, "I am going to join the Merchant Marines and make a lot of money so I can ask your mom for your hand in marriage."

I was blushing and laughing. "Are you serious?"

"Yes," said Robert, "I will mail you something from every port I visit. You may not hear from me for a while because the ships take petroleum through Russian territories. It is dangerous, but I want to make you rich."

He really meant what he said. He sent me beautiful things from all over the world. He then went to the Naval Academy and became an officer. Unfortunately, my feelings for him were not romantic, but more like the love between a brother and sister.

He came back rich and had a wonderful position, but we really never connected. He also went to the United States and became a doctor in Connecticut, where he was killed in a car accident, not far from me since I lived in Pennsylvania.

He told my parents that he loved America and this way he would be near me, in case I did not like it.

I was privileged enough to study English in school as my 3rd language. Every evening, prior to their rehearsal, two black musicians in the hotel near us who belonged to the big bands visited my parents and would spend an hour each day helping me with my English.

One lived in Coastville, PA, where he was a doctor, and the other lived in Ann Arbor, MI, where he was a lawyer. When they returned to the United States, they wrote me and I answered their letters, then they would correct all my mistakes, in red, and mail them back. They even sent us some care packages. (They were food packages) They helped me tremendously with the English language. That is how I was able to become an interpreter in the future. My friend Robert Rati was the biggest part of the fluency I mastered in the language.

By the end of the year, the American troops left France and went to Germany. They would remain there until 1948. Food was getting a little more plentiful now, but there was still no French bread in sight.

In the meantime, my Dad had to stay in Bar Le Duc for his job, and my Mom in Verdun. The separation was too much to bear for both of them; they decided to end their union. It had a terrible impact on my life. At the time, like many children, I did not understand their situation.

My mother was a very strong person and she continued her life with Arlette and me.

Germaine Esther Nanan
1919

*** The True Story of Monique Raguet/Jones ***

Identification card from NATO

General Eisenhower

162

Chapter 18: The Return of American Troops & the Birth of NATO

For the next two years, life slowly returned to normal. Our farmers' fields finally started to produce wheat. We could start making our precious French bread again.

The French army moved back in and occupied the barracks. French officers moved back into the building across from us on the other side of the river. Hair began to grow back on the heads of the unfortunate ladies who had it shaved, but many families were destroyed.

For some women, it was difficult to no longer be in charge of their household after four years of full responsibilities. They had been reunited with their husbands who were prisoners of war. They didn't know each other anymore. Personalities had changed. Many of our friends got divorced.

Some of the Jewish families that were taken away came back and reopened their businesses, but many of them never returned. They kept to themselves and looked very depressed, but we understood why later on. What they had gone through was so terrifying. One of those families had a younger son, another friend of Arlette, who had a <u>number</u> he received in the concentration camps <u>tattooed</u> on his arm.

"Arlette, I am so glad to be back home, I went through so much in the camps. I lost my family," he explained.

"Pierre, what happened over there?" my sister asked him.

He was in tears as he told us all the horrible things that he had to go through. I covered my ears so I couldn't hear, and I could not bear to see his arm. He told us how he had to crawl through a tunnel every week, and those who didn't make it through were shot by the Gestapo waiting at the other end with a rifle. I kept remembering how I had to take the breathing test every Saturday. It was bringing back very bad memories. He never smiled or laughed the whole time I knew him.

After everything settled down, the café was reopened and it was finally peaceful once again. We resumed our previous life. I played chess and bridge games with my college friends, some of our professors, and a few young French officers living at the Officers Club across the river. I became quite an expert in those games, but sports were not part of my curriculum, just the exercises that are still a good part of my life because the Germans had trained us in that direction.

One excellent chess player, I remember, was a professor in chemistry and a daily client whose family had roots in Germany. He would correspond each week with his German friend and make a chess move. The game lasted a few years. How interesting. Now we take those old fashioned ways of communication for granted with our Internet.

We also resumed going to the Opera House every week, located on the next block. My family is very fond of classical music, ballet, and operas. This beautiful building in Verdun is a replica of the "Opera House" in Paris, where the "Phantom of the Opera" was filmed. It is a magnificent chef d'oeuvre (work of art). The gallant soirees were conducted during the German occupation, but closed during the first few months of the Liberation due to the commotion caused by the interaction between the enemies and the allies.

I continued to go alone to our garden and do oil paintings. I liked to paint portraits of houses like Shakespeare's old house. I would spend hours there after school. It was my retreat. I was old enough for my mom to trust me. I had to paint the canvas, let it dry for a few days, then paint over it. A few of my works of art were framed and adorned the walls in our house. I regret not bringing some with me to the U.S. When I was finished with one, I would read classic literature like Racine, Chateaubriand, Musset, Moliere, Voltaire and many more.

One day, I was reading an English romance novel in which the name of the heroine was Patricia. I decided right then my first daughter would bear that name.

"Monique," Arlette once told me, "tonight on the Quai in front of our café **Edith Piaf** is going to sing (picture pg. 166)."

What a performance from this tiny little person all dressed in black who belted out her songs. Even now we listen to her CDs after all those years. Her performance was so poignant that we all wept. She is referred to as the *"little sparrow."* Some of her songs include *"La vie en rose."*

We were told the American troops were coming back. The new Army was much more polite and caring, respecting our way of life and feelings. They built new army barracks and even constructed a sports arena where I learned to appreciate boxing, which is no longer my favorite sport.

The engineering corps showed us how to build a bridge across the Meuse River in less than ten minutes. It was amazing how tanks could cross over the makeshift bridge immediately. The Tour de France, the biggest bicycle event in the world, also resumed and passed through Verdun on the Rue Mazel—it was so exciting!

Edith Piaf was a singer known world over

American swing bands came back and started playing for the U.S. officers. In our café, they mingled together with the French officers, which was so nice to see after what we went through. One day in our café, an American officer asked my mom if it would be okay for me to use my English skills. He was a friend of Robert Rati. I had to translate conversations between the officers from both countries on several occasions. Though I was proficient in English, my mother was outraged and didn't want me working for the army, but they promised they would pick me up in one of the army jeeps (that displayed a white star on its side) with a chauffeur who was a French lieutenant. They assured her they would take good care of me and followed a daily schedule.

He picked me up at 8:00 in the morning and brought me back by noon, then picked me up again at 2:00 and we returned at 6:00. Every morning and evening, we would salute the American flag right in the front of the window in my office.

At first, I translated for the people of my hometown in order to get them employment as switchboard operators, guards, hospital security, office workers and engineers. I believe every civilian native of Verdun came through me in order to get a job. I became very popular and it helped my mother's café.

Finally, we had all the positions filled and I was moved to the main building at the headquarters where all the officers from different countries were stationed. There was a young French lieutenant who was my personal secretary, and I was the interpreter for the French Liaison Colonel.

I spend an enormous amount of time with him, going to important sites translating, while my secretary did all the typing. It was a very rewarding challenge.

There is a big difference between being a translator and an interpreter. When you are a translator you have time to look up words, but an interpreter, as I was, is live description of the language. You have to bring up the intonation properly or the whole phrase is incorrect, and could cause an enormous disagreement. It is a very intense and demanding position, of course, only a young person would be able to pursue this career. I certainly would never be able to handle it now.

It was a great promotion, especially when I realized that I was working for the Embassy directly under General Eisenhower, and I was the third civilian to be hired (the other two were Germans). The Headquarter was in Fontainebleau a Chateau near Paris, but the second office was in my hometown. They occupied the building the French Officers used.

President Truman asked General Eisenhower, to go back to France after he finished his duties in Europe. His office was located in Fontainebleau. It was the birth of NATO. The General would come every week to our building in Verdun and sign our checks. Now looking back I should have kept one and not cashed it! We did not realize how important it would have been to keep one of my checks! It could have been a great souvenir and probably worth a lot of money today (especially since it was signed by Eisenhower himself). Working there was a wonderful job.

I am upset that I was too young to realize how influential my position was and the great moment in history of which I was a part of.

Chapter 19: My Wedding and My Few Remaining Months in France

While working for NATO, I met an American-born soldier who had participated in the Berlin Airlift. We were attracted to each other and kept bumping into one another. One day, after a few months, he took my mom and me for a ride to Bastogne. I received my engagement ring on top of the new monument erected in Bastogne. We climbed up the stairs to the top, but my mom decided to stay and wait for us at the bottom because it was too hard on her. He presented me with the ring while we were alone. That gesture was a real contradiction to my French upbringing. When we came down, I proudly showed my mom the ring. "Big mistake," she whispered.

I received the infamous "look." She then took me aside, pretending to admire the ring.

"What are you doing? That is not very polite. How are we going to announce the engagement now? I have a bad feeling about those Americans."

"Mom!" was all I could manage to say in response.

It became quite an involved relationship.

My mother was not in favor of my decision at first, but remembering the tragic circumstances following my sister's feelings for a Bavarian soldier and how it ended in tragedy, she was much more opened minded.

First, she insisted, the chaplain who was working at the American Embassy with us conduct an investigation on my future spouse's family. She wanted to be certain my future would be fine. However, I feel certain she was trying to discourage me. My 'to-be in-laws' neighbors were investigated in regard to their religion, morals, and standards in the community.

It became more complicated than we thought. The first step I had to take was to be approved by the American Army, and when the approval was accomplished, we had to apply for a civilian contract of marriage. The French law requires it. The mayor then had to approve it and we had to sign the papers in the courthouse. It took from Sept. 22nd until Oct. 2nd. During all those formalities, I had to share the bed with my mother at home, and my fiancé went back every night to the headquarters.

"You will be a virgin on your wedding day" my mother insisted. At that time, we did not get married in white if we were not virgins, at least in our circle.

Our wedding ceremony took place on Wednesday, October 2, 1951. In France, it is a tradition to wed during the week if you belong to the middle class, then you can afford to take the day off to celebrate. It was the first large French-American nuptial and was held in my cathedral.

As you entered this magnificent gothic church built above the catacombs, the air vibrated with the powerful religious music from a three-story high organ. It became the dream of every young girl from childhood.

The ceremony was conducted by three priests, one of which was our Bishop, a personal friend of our family, flanked by the only bilingual priest (who was studying at the seminary next to our church and spoke english) on his left and our parish priest on his right. At the beginning of the ceremony, the english-speaking priest came down toward us, holding a tiny gold tray. My future spouse proceeded to put money in it, but the priest whispered, "No, sir, we need the rings!" I did not dare look at my family but just smiled. What an embarrassing moment—he turned various shades of red. I felt badly for him because our customs are so different.

The magnitude of the music at the ceremony was surreal, in France, we do not play "Here Comes the Bride" as the bride strolls toward the altar, but classical music. She walks alone, not accompanied by her father or any other member of the family. On one side of the aisle were all French dignitaries and acquaintances; on the other side were the American officers I worked with in NATO. It was the first time a high mass was conducted in both languages. Many people from Verdun attended, some as friends, some just curious bystanders. Don't forget there were no American troops present for four years, so it was the first official international wedding. I was wearing a *"Coco Chanel"* designer's gown. It was a gorgeous dress with a long veil and train. I had "earned the right to wear white, my dear mom made sure of that.

I dreamed, as every bride does, about that moment where people take your photo and you feel like a princess. I had to rehearse how to walk and kneel on a velvet kneeler in the front of the altar, with the hoops inserted inside the enormous skirt. The first time, I didn't do very well and my dress lifted above my head while trying to kneel. I thought immediately, *I am in trouble.*

"*Monique, what are you doing? Every one is laughing at you!*" Arlette said with a grin of her face.

"Arlette, it is only the family," I answered, "and it is rehearsal time."

I felt so sorry for the ladies in the past who had to wear the hooped dresses.

Not much time was spent on those magical minutes coming out of church with bells ringing and friends applauding. Instead, my new spouse rolled my train and veil in his arms and pushed me into the limo. He was rude and I was very upset, my family extremely hurt, and so were our friends

Again, I saw "the look" from the corner of my teary eyes. I was devastated, but kept quiet.

Afterward, we had our dinner reception in the exclusive restaurant called "*Le Coq Hardy*" located on the street in front of the Monument de la Victoire, where each waiter is appointed to just four customers.

The outside of Le Coq Hardy

The Inside

Monique in NATO

The dinner lasted four hours, and with each course we had a different wine. The dishes would be replaced continuously, and the servers made certain our wine glasses were always half filled with the proper wine. It is another French custom. The wedding cake is also very different, made from *"choux"* (small éclairs) arranged in the form of a pyramid with different kinds of nuts and held together by a hard caramel sauce. The dinner is concluded by a glass of champagne, *but without clanging on glasses for kissing!*

Another embarrassing moment occurred when we left the restaurant, went home to change our clothes, then got into our automobile; tin cans were attached to the back of the car and rattled behind us, as we drove away. All the townspeople were laughing they were unfamiliar with the American way of celebrating newlyweds.

My parents were mortified again; it was not French. I realized I would have to face many more hardships in the future.

Upon my return from our honeymoon in Switzerland, cut extremely short since my husband was bored! I continued working for NATO until I came to America.

After spending Thanksgiving in France, a holiday which we do not observe, but we found it wonderful, for the first time we had a Turkey dinner we purchased at the PX (store for Army and their families) and all the trimmings. Again our company at the table was international. We thought it was a wonderful family tradition.

We also spent Christmas in Verdun, and for the first time had a "Sapin de Noel" (Christmas tree). We always put out our annual very ornate nativity set. It was kind of magical to see all the lights on the tree. Christmas trees are a German tradition, not French. We went, as custom demands it, to the midnight mass, then after the ceremony sat for a five hour dinner, plenty of food especially prepared for the occasion and drinks. It is called the "Réveillon." Christmas in France was strictly religious and not dedicated to children, they received their toys on St. Nicholas's Day, December 7th.

After the diner we all went to bed, around 6 AM. At noon, the sirens went off, as they did every day to make sure they were still in working condition. I got up immediately without thinking and went to my chair, got dressed and went downstairs. It was an automatic response to the sirens; I guess it was another reminder of those war times.

Where are you going Monique? I heard from my family. We were staying in my mother's house.

I was still shaking, and had a flash back of the incredible noise caused by planes invading the sky, hundreds at one time, like black birds, one against the other. I understand now, why I could never watch the movie "The Birds" directed by Alfred Hitchcock. It reminded me of those black bombers, it was a terrible horrifying sensation. We felt like death was surrounding us, then we had the wonderful feeling *"we escape another day"*.

My spouse was called back to the United States at the beginning of February 1952, and my parents purchased my ticket for the trip on the Queen Elizabeth. They did not want me to sail on an army ship.

The Duke & Duchess of Windsor
(Former King of England)

Queen Elizabeth in harbor

*** The True Story of Monique Raguet/Jones ***

R.M.S. "Queen Elizabeth" Friday, February 29, 1952

PROGRAMME OF EVENTS
— :o: —

A.M.

7.00 to 7.00 p.m.—Swimming Pool and Gymnasium available

9.30—Cinema : Film entitled   Theatre
   " JUST THIS ONCE "
   Janet Leigh and Peter Lawford

11.00—Gymnasium Classes   Gymnasium

11.15—Gerry Kavanagh at the Hammond Organ   Main Lounge
   (Relayed)

11.45—Boat Drill for Cherbourg Passengers   Promenade Deck
   All Passengers are requested to attend wearing lifebelts

P.M.

2.00—Cinema : Film entitled   Theatre
   " JUST THIS ONCE "
   Janet Leigh and Peter Lawford

3.30—Melody Time   Main Lounge
   Gerry Kavanagh at the Organ (relayed)

4.00—Music for Tea Time   Main Lounge
   Lew Riley and the "Queen Elizabeth" Orchestra

5.00—Recorded Concert   Main Lounge
   Symphony No. 4 in G Major (Op. 88 (Dvorak)
   The Philadelphia Orchestra. Conductor: Rafael Kubelik

6.00—Cocktail Hour   Cocktail Bar

8.00—Recorded Musical Selections   Main Lounge

8.45—" The Voice of America "—News Broadcast   Main Lounge

9.00—B.B.C. News Broadcast   Main Lounge

9.15—Keno (Housie-Housie or Bingo)   Main Lounge
   Followed by a "GET TOGETHER" DANCE
   Lew Riley and the "Queen Elizabeth" Orchestra

A.M.

1.00—The "Elizabethan Club"   Smoke Room and Cocktail Bar
   The "Queen Elizabeth" Trio   Dancing until 3 a.m.

Itinerary for *Queen Elizabeth*

The Duke and Duchess of Windsor were also traveling on this ship, returning from the funeral of King George VI of England, the oldest son who abdicated the throne as King Edward VIII, in order to marry an American divorcee, Wallis Simpson. He then became the Duke of Windsor. It was the beginning of a new era for *Queen Elizabeth II* the King's daughter and heir; and a new beginning for me.

After looking back on my life over the years, I'm proud of the experiences I have encountered. I want to teach others about an era we all seem to have forgotten. History is rewarding people should know the true facts and not listen to the fiction they hear in stories and movies. I only trust my personal involvement. I hope that someday everyone will realize that we are all the same and we all desire peace.

Other French citizens had different interpretations of the war, especially the privileged ones who lived in the unoccupied zone in the South of France. I found out years later by reading books that half of my country did not go through the hunger and fear everyday as we did.

When I came to the United States of America, I was devoted to my family and raised my three children, but I had to resign from my prestigious position which I still regret. It was very sad that I was not able to pursue my childhood dreams. But I am so grateful now to be able to teach my native tongue and share my past with my French students, who convinced me to write this book.

One door closes, but another one opens. We are now enduring years of insecurity and disturbing world wide events, so please think about the children whose lives are or will be deeply affected by War all over the world.

I was blessed and saved by God so many times as He took me under his wing. He also gave me the courage to face my memories and finally write about them.

I now understand why my mom was so different from my dad. They were raised in opposite sides of France: the North, which was always under the pressure of war; and the South, full of happiness and sunshine. I have such an enormous respect and admiration for her after writing my memories of the ordeal she went through which brought many long-forgotten situations to the surface.

This book is in your memory, Mom, out of enormous love and gratitude for your courage..

THE END

In my next book I will speak of a Lampeter Strasburg Middle School Principal for whom I worked in Lancaster, PA. He had the privileged to be one of the MP'S present at the trial of Nuremberg for General Goering, Hitler's right hand. The principal, Mr., George Myers was a friend of the Chaplain who recalled in writing the last minutes of the Goering's life. Quite an exceptional ending.

*** The True Story of Monique Raguet/Jones ***

Hitler and Officers

Acknowledgements

Special thanks to my wonderful husband Paul Boyer Jones, Jr., whose encouragement and support helped me through the writing, editing and emotions that this book created in me.

My immense gratitude also goes to my friend Grant A. Durier Miller, for his contributions to the writing of the book as well as his overall support during the entire process. I could not have accomplished it without him.

I wish to thank all my students whose support, kind words and encouragement meant more to me than they will ever realize.

Father Ward with his knowledge of the War since he was an air force colonel

Father Michael Grebb for his moral support.

*** The True Story of Monique Raguet/Jones ***

I hope the story of my youth will help and encourage my three wonderful children with difficulties they might encounter in their lives. A Mother's love and best wishes for her children is always in her heart.

Also to all those poor innocent children who have to endure similar circumstances, my heart and understanding are with you.

*All photos except for Raguet's family photos courtesy of Wikipedia; all maps courtesy of Google
**Some names have been changed to protect identity of acquaintances involved in story

*** WWII Through the Eyes of a Child ***